three◯ **Project Solutions Inc.**

PRESENTS

HOW TO DOCUMENT A PROJECT PLAN:

WHAT YOU NEED TO KNOW TO DESIGN A PROJECT MANAGEMENT PLAN QUICKLY AND EASILY

By
Glen Ford, PMP

Published By
*Training*NOW
Mississauga, Canada

Sale of this book without a cover may be unauthorized. If this book is without a cover, it may have been reported as unsold and destroyed. Neither the publisher nor the author will have been paid for their efforts.

© 2011, Glen Ford and TrainingNOW

Published by TrainingNOW, Mississauga & Oakville, Ontario, Canada
http://www.TrainingNOW.ca
http://www.LearningCreators.com
"Presents" imprint and associated logo used with permission,
Logo in "Presents" imprint © Three O Project Solutions Inc.,
Toronto, Ontario, Canada. http://threeo.ca

ISBN (Kindle Edition): 978-0-9867885-5-0
ISBN (Print Edition) : 978-0-9867885-4-3

PMP®, *PMBOK® Guide*, PMI® and several other related registered marks used throughout this book are registered marks of the Project Management Institute, Newton Square, PA, USA.

R20131127.103900

For Raymond Ford,

1929 — 2011

who read me my first book.

"Lady was the mother,
Tramp was the father ..."

Acknowledgements

No book is ever created just by its author. Many people had a hand in this book's creation. I would especially like to thank the following people.

To my wife Lisa. Who has put up with me through the long days (and sometimes nights) as I learned to perfect my art. And then put up with me while I turned that art to building companies and finally to writing and teaching. Who sometimes fed me, and often carried me. I may not say it, but I really do know what you've gone through for me.

To my son Dafydd and daughter Solenne, who have taught me the true meaning of herding cats. And the joy to be found in helping people to achieve their dreams.

To my late father who taught me, guided me and pushed me. I owe you more than I can ever say.

To my former partners at VProz, Greg Plonka and Tony Araujo for their feedback during the writing of this book. And of course, putting up with me at VProz.

To Paul Benson and my friends at TrainingNOW for their support and efforts in dragging this book from concept to published work.

I hope that you enjoy this book and that it proves to be useful to you. Project Management is a profession that easily leads to bureaucracy and yet the fastest way to destroy its purpose is with the very bureaucracy it can create. With this book I hope to strip away some of the bureaucracy while still maintaining the integrity of the activities and documentation needed to successfully manage projects. I hope this book helps you to achieve your project management goals.

Could you take five minutes to help in return?

Other readers rely on your opinions when choosing which books to spend their precious time reading. Writers like me rely on your feedback to improve their writing and to know what topics to write about next.

If you enjoyed this book, please express your rating and opinions on Amazon. Amazon provides a facility for rating and reviewing on the page where you purchased this book. You can reach the review page by going to the bottom of http://www.amazon.com/dp/B005YV7BTS and selecting the 'write a customer review' button.

On the other hand, if you didn't enjoy this book or if you want me to write about other topics, please let me know directly. You can do so through the contact form available at my publisher's site http://TrainingNOW.ca or the one at my own website http://GlenDFord.com/. While you are at my site, feel free to check out my blog. It contains many of my thoughts on project management, innovation and business management for entrepreneurs.

Thank You and Enjoy!

Glen Ford

TrainingNOW Books By Glen Ford

How to Write Your Own How-To EBook in 24 Hours or Less:
The information products secret revealed!

How to Document a Project Plan: What you need to know to design a
project management plan quickly and easily

How to Blog for Money: 9 strategies to get your blog earning money online
and off

Writer's Block Demolition: Finding the time to write, keeping writing, and
finish YOUR book

101 Writing Tweets: 101 tips and tweets about writing how-to books for the
Kindle

As Glen Douglas

How To Build A Raised Garden Bed

With Paul Benson

101 Limericks About Public Speaking

Contents

Chapter 1:

Projects, Plans And Preparation

How Not To Sail A Tall Ship

Let me tell you a story.

When I was younger, single and had more money, I travelled a great deal. It was my only real vice. I travelled to Europe. I travelled throughout North America. I travelled throughout the Caribbean. I even managed to reach Africa! Or at least I brought back a rug from Morocco that still hangs on my wall.

One of my trips was a cruise in the Caribbean with Windjammer's Barefoot Cruises. Now, for those of you who aren't familiar with this line, they converted a number of tall ships to passenger ships. The tall ship I sailed on was the 248 foot, 430 ton S.V. Polynesia. As the "Argus", she was one of the last of the Portuguese Grand Banks schooners. Beautiful wood. Expanses of white sails. And very hard bunks. In exchange for comfort, passengers received many times that value in sheer experiences. From hoisting the sail, to diving off the deck, to scuba diving lessons. And a few that I'm not going to share where my kids can hear! (I'd heard of shampooing with beer before, but showering?).

One of the experiences I had was to steer this great ship for the better part of an evening shift. We were sailing a channel between two islands. So of course, we were buffeted by the currents. The waves would roll in from the Atlantic, bounce against one island, then bounce against its mate. And in between, the poor ship would be pushed first one way then back the other.

Not having experience in anything larger than a 20-foot racer, I valiantly tried to maintain a perfect magnetic heading. I even became quite good at predicting the next push off course! Meanwhile, the poor helmsman behind me kept saying over and over, "You're not driving a car. You're not driving a car."

Many years later, I was working as a project management consultant trying to explain the concepts behind project management. That's when the light finally came on. I finally realized what that poor misunderstood sailor was trying to tell me. A sailing ship of that size doesn't willingly change course. It goes straight. It fixes a course and goes that way. It doesn't turn quickly. And it doesn't turn easily. My quick adjustments weren't really having any effect!

A business is very much like that large sailing ship.

On a sailing ship, the captain and the navigator decide where the ship is going to go. The ship, the engine and the screws (or the sails, in the Polynesia's case) move the ship, crew and cargo. However, they only do so in a straight line. Left to themselves they go in whatever direction they happen to be pointed. Regardless of the desires of the captain! It takes the combined efforts of the helmsman, the helm and the rudder to adjust the ship so it's pointed in the right direction.

A business, no matter the size, is much like that sailing ship. The strategic managers (usually the CEO and senior executive) determine where they want the business to go. But the business itself, the operations, doesn't necessarily want to go there. By their nature, operational departments want to continue doing exactly what they are doing today. They are pointed in one direction and that is exactly where they are going!

To move this great ship you need a helmsman, helm and rudder to apply pressures to adjust the path of the behemoth. In business, this combination is the strategic project.

Strategic projects exist to change the direction of an organization.

What Is A Project And Why Would I Want To Plan It?

What Is A Project?

The Project Management Institute (PMI) defines a project as "a temporary endeavor undertaken to create a unique product, service or result". A project has a definite beginning, a definite end and a definite objective. While it may use standard processes, it needs to combine them in unique ways in order to create that unique result. While it may last a long time (or a short time), it does start and it does end. It doesn't go on forever.

But this definition doesn't say enough. For that, we need to define three other terms.

The first is the concept of an operational or tactical project. These are projects whose objectives are focused on an operational result. In other words, keeping the lights on and doing more of the same thing -- just a little better. For example, replacing an obsolete software program with the latest and greatest. Or even better, installing the latest release of that program. They tend to be simple, involve only a few people and only one or two skill sets. Sometimes these are referred to as program-based projects since programs (or programmes if you live in Europe) carry out their operations by this type of project. *(Ed: You've confused me, what does software have to do with projects? Glen: Grrrr – I hate English. Program or programme as in Government funding. Operations being run as a project. Or a super-project being run as an operation.)*

The second is the concept of a strategic project. These are projects whose objective is specifically intended to move the organization towards a strategic goal. Their focus is changing the direction of operations. In short, giving the operations new goals. One strategic initiative may require several projects to achieve that goal. Or it may involve only one project.

The third concept you need to understand is that of the project portfolio. An organization can only do so many things. It has limits on its money, on the number of people it can attract, and on other resources. These limits restrict the number of projects that are possible. Some projects cannot be done with the resources available. This means that an organization needs to manage which projects it is going to do and when.

At its simplest, a project portfolio is simply the list of all the projects an organization can do, should do or intends to do.

What Makes A Project Succeed?

As a project management professional, I'm often frustrated at what most business people think makes a project succeed.

To be successful in an operational portion of the business, it is necessary for the manager to know the bits and pieces of that portion of operations. In effect, he or she needs to be an expert in the subject their department deals with. That's partially why companies are organized functionally. And also why the myth of the "Manager Who Knows All" arose.

Unfortunately, many people believe that being a subject matter expert is important for a project manager as well. After all, projects are just short-term operational jobs, aren't they?

In fact, while having a subject matter expert (SME) on a project is important, all but the smallest operational project requires multiple SMEs. In short, unless you are prepared to hire a multi-faceted Renaissance man (or woman), the chances of finding someone with the perfect skill set is impossible. Take a construction project, for example. There are over five different types of carpenters involved in a house project. Finding one person with skills and knowledge in all the types of carpentry is unlikely. And that's just one trade. Finding a project manager with skills in electrical, plumbing, carpentry and all the other trades and all the sub-trades isn't going to happen.

So if super-human skill isn't a source of success in projects, what is?

Statistics from failed projects give us the three answers. The first answer lies in the science of project management. These are those tools and techniques you need to know to plan and manage a project. These skills provide the factual base to everything that comes after.

The second answer is the ability to build a temporary team, manage that team, manage expectations and manage relationships with the various stakeholders. This is the art of project management. When handled correctly, it causes a project to finish effectively and efficiently.

The third source of project success lies within the first two answers. All projects will take as long as they will take. And they will cost as much as they will cost. And they will produce exactly what they are designed to produce. The key to success lies in ensuring that the right project is being done. And determining, in advance, if the right project is even possible.

That's the purpose of planning.

So How Do You Guarantee Success?

A project plan is a key element in creating a successful project. It does three things for you:

1. It identifies what must happen to succeed
2. It predicts what will happen.
3. It helps ensure that desires meet the reality test.

In short, more projects fail because they were designed to fail than for any other reason. They did not succeed because they could not succeed.

A project plan helps you avoid failure by giving you the information needed to bring expectations and reality into alignment. They provide a necessary check to make sure that your path is the correct one. Or at least as far as you can tell, based on the information you have when you start the project.

Traditional Philosophy And The Holistic Philosophy?

Different project managers have different opinions as to what is important in project management. This philosophy affects their entire view of project management, their understanding and their actions when managing projects. It also affects the plans they develop.

The Traditional Philosophy

The traditional philosophy (for our purposes at least) is based on four different elements.

1. A focus on the science of project management

2. A focus on the bureaucratic aspects
3. A focus on management expectations
4. A battle for control between methodologies.

In the traditional philosophy there is a focus on the science of project management. As much as people try to pretend they focus on the people aspects. And as much as they might promote the need to manage people not the project. The science of project management remains their highest priority. The plan, the reports and the project documents are the most important output of a project.

It's inevitable that this focus on the science of project management should also be accompanied by a focus on the paperwork. After all, much of the science is expressed through forms and writing.

Much of this bureaucracy is going to be focused on providing information to the management team. It is management that demands and justifies the paperwork after all. It is inevitable that a project manager's first job is to manage the expectations of both the manager and stakeholders.

If one focuses on the science of project management then inevitably one will create a project management methodology. Ways and means, tools and techniques for managing projects. And of course, your method is always better than the other guy's. The result is an argument between proponents of different styles of project management.

Let's take an example from information systems development. At the moment, there are two major camps in methodology.

Waterfall methodology believes that the systems development life cycle should be the basis of your project. You finish the requirements phase. Then you go on to the design phase. And so on. Each phase is distinct and you "never" go back more than one phase. Of course, mistakes happen and a project manager needs to be flexible. But that's the basis of the methodology. The project finishes each step and then goes on to the next. Never going back. Never repeating. Documentation is key. Change is a foe to be managed. It's like building a house. Each phase must be complete before the next can begin. Otherwise the roofers get wet cement on their boots.

The Agile philosophy is much more organic. You begin with a general understanding and a fixed number of "sprints" of a fixed time period. Each of these mini-projects set their own priorities. Each is responsible for identifying what it will do, and what the requirements are. Change is at the root of the process and largely unmonitored. Documentation is the enemy. It's like a puzzle party. Each person picks a corner, assembles what they can and then integrates it into the whole.

It's inevitable that two radically different philosophies disagree. The Agile camp dismisses the Waterfall camp as backwards and rigid. While the Waterfall camp dismisses the Agile camp as frivolous and risky.

The Holistic Philosophy

On the other hand the Holistic philosophy is focused on trying to take into account all the forces that affect a project. As a result, it proposes:

1. That a balanced focus on the art and science of project management is critical for success.
2. Keeping the paperwork as simple as possible.

3. That managing expectations isn't enough, you also need to manage how people react to the inevitable change in their routine.
4. That different projects have different key success factors and therefore need different methods.

For the follower of the holistic view, the science of project management is important. In fact, having an understanding of the planning process is mandatory. Arguably, the art of project management is even more important. In order for a project to succeed you must have the art down pat. It's just that to succeed with the art you must also have the science down. Action based on knowledge and skill as it were.

This belief in the balance of the art and science also leads to an attitude that can best be described as "Just Enough Paperwork". You need some paperwork. Paperwork is a good thing, in fact. If well designed, it can even help you ensure that you cover all the bases and complete tasks in the right order. The key is not to forget that the paperwork is a means to an end -- not an end in and of itself!

Similarly, a holistic philosophy also leads to the belief that control is mandatory. However, the nature of the control changes from project to project. In effect, corporate requirements for the project should determine the methodology used. Both Agile and Waterfall methods have their place. Success with any methodology is a case of selecting the right methods for the right project.

Agile, for example, works well in projects involving high degrees of uncertainty. Or in projects where fulfilling the full scope of the project mandate is far less important than delivering something in the given amount of time and within the budget. In these cases, the use of a set number of semi-independent sprints is a much better technique. Each sprint is effectively its own project. Each determines what it will do and what it needs to know to do it. The use of a fixed number of exploratory cycles is well suited to a project where the result cannot be clearly visualized.

On the other hand, can you imagine building a bridge that way? Each support being built only as high as you can get in the given budget. Only the amount of asphalt being used as can be completed in the given time. Projects where the scope is more important than time or budget are perfect candidates for the Waterfall method. The stepped nature of waterfall methodologies is better suited to the nature of projects where design must be done up front in order to reduce rework or to ensure overall quality.

However, reverse this and use an Agile methodology on a fixed scope variable time & money project. The result won't be pretty. Or use a Waterfall methodology when you can only generally identify requirements and you have a limited budget.

The most important element of the holistic philosophy however, is the realization that there is more to the people side than just the management of expectations. Your project, especially if it is strategic, is going to change the environment for some or all of your stakeholders. To succeed your project needs to incorporate their reaction to those changes. Your project plan must incorporate methods to overcome negative reactions. Equally, your project must take into account their reasons for objecting to the change. After all, resistance to change is a defense mechanism intended to prevent us from making mistakes.

This latter philosophy underlies much of what you will find in the following pages.

What This Book Is About

In this book I'm going to perform a business systems analysis -- sometimes called a "business process analysis" --

on the initiation stages of project management. This stage produces what is often referred to as a project plan or project manual or even a project plan manual. In any case, it covers the planning of the project and the preparation of the main documents which describe how the project will be performed -- the project plan. It begins with asking the project manager to take on the task and ends with the agreement of all parties of what will be done.

Since our focus is on what documents are required I am not going to describe the tasks that need to be performed but rather focus on major task groups which produce the document. For example, risk management actually consists of several steps:

1. Plan Risk Management Strategy
2. Identify Risks
3. Perform Qualitative Risk Analysis
4. Perform Quantitative Risk Analysis
5. Plan Risk Responses

However, for our purposes they all form a high-level task we have called "risk analysis".

Similarly, space limitations in this book have forced me to focus on only those aspects of documentation produced during the planning of the project. Many other documents are produced during the execution, management and closing of the project. In many cases, the paperwork associated with these processes can be combined with the outputs of the planning process. However, as I will discuss later, combining the outputs of different tasks groups within the project often results in a misunderstanding of the nature of each task group.

A Word About Computerization Of Project Plans

There is an old saying that "the cobbler's children often go barefoot". As a key part of IT, project managers often feel like those poor children. Quite frankly, the software varies from highly detailed to barely existing. And from high quality to a "will this work this time or not?" experience in frustration. Everyone who writes a project management package has a different opinion of what needs to be included. And the software reflects that difference.

Rather than turn this book into a product manual, I have made the decision to avoid the issue altogether. I'm far more interested in improving your general skill than teaching a particular software product. Besides -- everyone can picture a paper manual and not everyone will be able to picture the software product I happen to use. Finally, paper is the easiest media to change. Software changes involve databases, analysts, programmers, quality assurance and so forth. Paper involves a typewriter (that's what word processors used to be) and piece of paper. Maybe some whiteout!

Finally, not all project managers have access to computer support. The promise of a paperless office has not permeated the world. All you have to do is look at my desk to realize that! So most project managers will -- at one point or another -- have to create or use a paper project manual.

So for all these reasons, I'm going to proceed as though we were creating a paper project manual. But everything I say can (and should) be adapted for computerized project manuals.

An Offer Of Free Templates

One of the problems with writing a book such as this one is that many people have problems visualizing the physical based on a conceptual description. In this particular case, that means people may read this book but be unable to turn the book into a set of forms. The obvious solution would be to include templates in the book. Unfortunately, the electronic version of this book really isn't designed to display letter-sized templates. I have two solutions for this problem.

You can find the first solution toward the end of the book. I have added a sample project plan manual to the GlenDFord.com website. You can find the actual address at the end of this book. By reviewing a simple plan, you can identify what your plan should look like.

The second solution is also in the form of a download. In this solution, I remove the need to visualize the form. That's right: I have a set of project templates for you to download from the web. You will find directions near the end of the book. These templates are free for you to modify for your own needs and use.

Chapter 2

Before You Start

How To Destroy A Project In One Easy Step

A good project management process is a very powerful force for changing the organization. It's like the helmsman, helm and rudder for the ship. But, like that assembly, if out of step or improperly assembled, it can just as easily be a force for failure. Imagine if the rudder chain was connected backwards. (And yes, this has really happened).

I remember working with a former client many years ago. The engagement was as a business analyst on an IT project rather than in my usual project management consultant role. And I was looking forward to working with them with a mix of fear and eagerness.

You see, they were a major force in their business. And a major employer of consultants in an industry that was known to use consultants extensively. But they had developed a bad reputation amongst the consultants they employed.

When I showed up at the site, the first task I was given was to take a series of courses on how the company worked and what it expected. A course and manual on how they wanted a project run quickly followed. I was ecstatic! Finally, a company that knew how to run a project! Or so I believed.

It didn't take long for me to realize that the team that created their methodology hadn't really understood the purpose of the artifacts they created. They'd never performed a business analysis on the tasks in order to understand what was being done and why. As a result, they'd institutionalized laziness on the part of their management. They'd merged several documents and then misnamed them. But that was a common mistake and at the time, I ignored it.

Then I started the project.

Now, I had been brought in well into the project in order to backfill for a consultant "who got a better offer" and had left. At the time, that was a common market trend and I didn't think anything about it. However, I soon realized that the project was really in severe trouble.

The first task I was given was to help the project team (or steering committee as they called it), develop a document which they mistakenly called a project charter. I found that rather hard to believe at the time. Charters are produced by the sponsor -- at least in theory. And they are produced before the project begins. And I knew for a fact, that the programming staff was in the middle of testing the solution. So what were they producing?

As it turns out, that was exactly the situation.

You see the methodology had accepted that VPs would not bother to document their orders. So their methodology combined the response from the project team (the project plan) with the charter and then called it a charter. After all, the project manager was going to have to document both things, weren't they.

Now bring in a project team that didn't understand project management at all. However, they did understand politics and avoiding responsibility. By the time they finished debating what they would take responsibility for, the programmers had gotten worried they couldn't finish in time. So using their best guess the programmers had gone off and done what they had to do. Fortunately, it was simple enough that they didn't need direction.

There are several lessons to learn from this project. I mean beyond the fact that killing a project is sometimes the only way to get the project back under control. And that politics is a quick way to sink a project.

Learning Not To Destroy Projects

Firstly, it is important to understand why the documents exist. Names are important. Especially when it comes to generally accepted forms mentioned in "A Guide to the Project Management Body of Knowledge" (a project management standard better known as the *PMBOK® Guide*). Combining and repurposing forms can be okay. However, then calling them by a standardized "professional" name can cause people to misunderstand the purpose of the document. Especially when the purpose of the "standardized" document is so often misunderstood by those professionals.

The earlier that mistake is made, the more extensive the error becomes as people who are less expert begin to work the procedures. (And of course, those who are more expert begin to ignore the procedures). Changing the names of the documents to a more obvious terminology is an easy way to overcome this. Of course, then you'll need to map the name to the term from the *PMBOK® GUIDE*.

The second lesson is not to confuse who really does the work with who should have been doing the work. In the real world, busy people often dump documents off on other people. That doesn't mean they aren't responsible for the paperwork. Only that the other person is doing the work.

If I apply business process (aka business systems) analysis skills to project management, I get an initiation task that looks like figure 1.

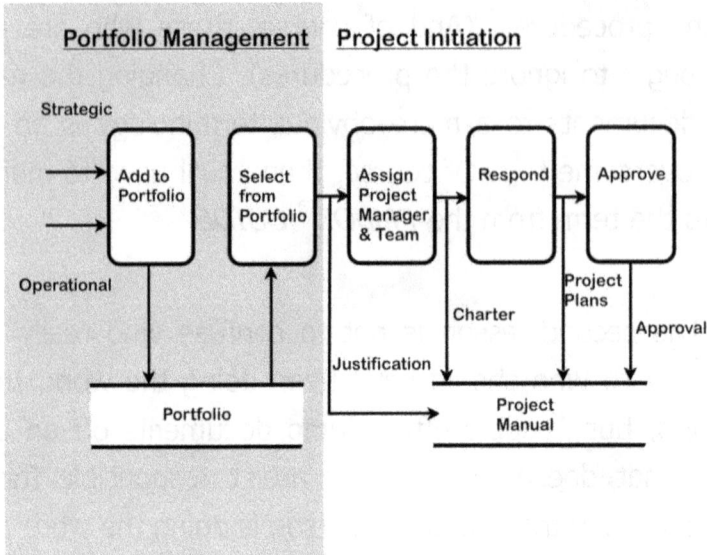

Figure 1

Cutting the project initiation process down to the minimum it consists of:

1. The sponsor assigns a project manager
2. The assignment form (the Charter) and the related request information from the Portfolio (i.e. the Justification and Portfolio description) are stored.
3. The project manager (and his team) prepares a response describing how they will actually accomplish the assignment. This is the project plan.
4. This proposal (the project plan) is stored with the assignment form and justification and sent to the sponsor.

5. The sponsor reviews the proposal and authorizes the project to proceed as planned.
6. The approval or authorization is combined with the rest of the information and becomes the directions for the team actually performing the work.

Of course, in the real world things become confused. Terms are changed (request becomes charter becomes statement of work becomes work package). People who do the actual work changes (the sponsor doesn't want to fill in a form so the project manager fills the Charter in). Tasks are performed at the same time or in the wrong order. As a result, the documents lose their separate identity (the charter and the project plan become confused as in the story that began this chapter). Or approval is given before the project plan has been prepared. (This is so commonplace a mistake that people accept it without even stopping long enough to recognize just how silly it is).

The diagram above agrees with the standard assignment process (assign, respond, approve) and is the logic behind the initiation phase. No matter how you re-slot elements or re-assign them or completely forget them, this is what you are really trying to do.

The *PMBOK® Guide*'s Philosophy

As I've mentioned so far, terminology and practices can vary considerably. Even the standards for best practices can drift off the track due to the variations.

For example, the Project Management Institute (PMI), which is generally considered the industry registrar in North America, heads off into the wilds with its terminology occasionally.

While much of the rest of the practical world believes that the project plan is the schedule, the *PMBOK® Guide* overcorrects that mistake. Within its framework, the initiation phase produces two document sets:

- The Project Plan

- The Project Documents

The project plan is considered the statement of the processes the project will follow. In essence, it is the strategy and procedures document. That's fine as far as it goes. However, PMI goes on to separate the other outputs of project planning and calls them simply project documents. So the schedule and risk register for example -- two key documents in the plans -- are actually considered not to be part of the project plan.

Similarly, the *PMBOK® Guide* implies, at least, that the procedures and strategy for each project will be unique for the project. As a result, several procedures documents form part of the Project Plan. This despite the fact that these procedures are often standardized throughout the organization. And the inclusion of so much paper almost guarantees that no one will read the project plan.

Projects In Real Life

In real life, most projects do not operate in isolation. While some procedures need to be hunted down and identified, many are fixed in the collective mind of the organization's management. Rather than expecting an analysis and re-design of the company's policies, management is expecting the plans to only include strategies and variations on the standard procedures necessitated by the project.

Similarly, most managers expect the plans to include any output from the planning process. This is especially true of the schedule -- which in many cases is the only thing they care about. In fact, as I've mentioned, many managers consider the schedule to be the whole project plan. While that's somewhat foolish for many reasons, it is a far more common opinion than is appropriate. It needs to be treated as a common misconception.

The Philosophy In This Book And Some Notes On Terminology

In this book, I'm going to meet both PMI and the general public in the middle. Hey, I'm Canadian! What else would you expect? While I agree with the *PMBOK® Guide* on what is required and what is output in detail, I'm going to agree with general public opinion as to what is included in the plan. Anything output by the planning process and used either to support the approval or to direct the project belongs as part of the project plan document (which I'm referring to as the project manual).

On the other hand, I'm going to disagree with the *PMBOK® Guide* and support the real world with regards to procedures. In fact, the next section of this chapter is directly concerned with pre-defined procedures. There are certain procedures you must have in place before you start any project. While projects may vary from those procedures, it is important to follow those procedures. Any variances must be justified. This allows you to both react and yet, be able to improve the project management processes.

In addition, I have rather arbitrarily chosen to use certain terminology and avoid other terms. For example, I use the term Charter to refer to the document assigning the project manager and the team to the project. A number of other terms are also in common use (both by the public and the *PMBOK® Guide*).

Similarly, I use the term Project Plan to refer to the outputs of the planning (or response) process as a whole. This includes a number of sub-plans including the risk plan, the communications plan and so on. Unfortunately, the term project plan also refers to the document that combines the project plan, the Charter and the justification document used in the portfolio. Typically, these plans are also stored separately in a binder called the project manual. I have therefore used the term project plan to refer to the outputs of the planning process, and project manual to refer to the document submitted for approval.

It should be noted that this latter definition will break down outside of the initiation phase. Unfortunately, the project manual typically contains the ongoing reporting and revised documents in later phases. However, as this book doesn't deal with anything outside of initiation, I'll leave that issue to later books to resolve.

The *PMBOK® Guide* And This Book

As you read through this book, you may get the impression that I don't think very highly about the *PMBOK® Guide* Nothing could be further from the truth. Like most project management professionals (including most PMP® Credential Holders) there are elements of the *PMBOK® Guide* I disagree with. But those are largely professional differences of opinion.

The *PMBOK® Guide* is a framework around which can be built professional and organizational knowledge. Its focus is on building project management and promoting best practices. To do so frequently requires the *PMBOK® Guide* to leave the real world behind and enter the world of theory.

My objective is not so grandiose.

My objective in this book is to describe the documentation that a project manager requires -- as a minimum -- in order to fully document his plans for the project. This means I'm going to simplify, reorganize, and rethink much of the *PMBOK® Guide*. In short, I'm going to add a healthy dose of reality to it. Along the way I'm going to compare the *PMBOK® Guide* to what happens in real life. Quite frankly, it's not fair to do that but then again life isn't fair!

The Task Assignment Cycle

Underlying all the elements of the project initiation phase is the concept of the task assignment cycle. After all, that's what the initiation phase is task assignment.

The task assignment cycle is a model (meaning a description of the real world) of how to be successful when assigning tasks. Sound familiar?

Assignment Cycle

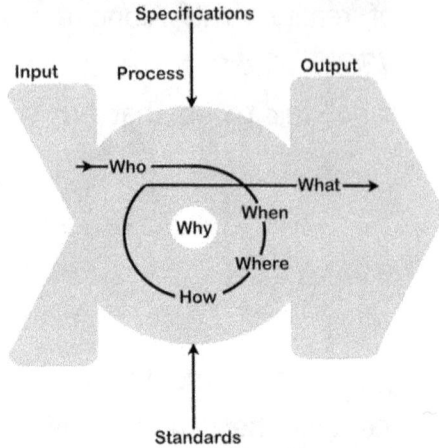

Specifications

Input   Process   Output

Who

What

When

Why

Where

How

Standards

Figure 2

A fancy version looks like the picture in Figure 2.

The simple version says that in order to be successful, you need people to know:

- Who is doing the work

- When they need to get it done

- Where they need to get it done (if applicable)

- How they should do it

- What they need to do

- And most of all WHY they are doing it

There are two important things to remember about the list. The first is that everything revolves around the "WHY?" question. People must understand the context and reasoning behind what they are doing. Otherwise, they will make mistakes. The second is that once a person is trained on the how, a good manager will let their people make the how decisions on their own. That's one definition of a high efficiency team.

Chapter 3

Before Any Project Starts

The Role Of A PMO

When I started to write this section, I wasn't sure if I was being rather pretentious. After all, there are many different types of Project Management Office. Every organization has a different need. And the PMO fulfills a different role. Some organizations have a single PMO for the whole organization. Others have separate PMOs for each part of the company. Still others only have a PMO in heavy project areas such as IT. And that doesn't even begin to address the fact that some companies outsource the PMO role to companies from small Project Management boutique-style consultants to large multi-national, multi-functional Mega-consulting goliaths that will take over your whole business for you if you ask.

How could I possibly say -- this is what your PMO needs to be?

But in fact, no matter what the overall role the PMO fulfills, there is one role that the PMO must take on in order for projects to succeed. Before any project in your organization begins, two things must be in place for projects to succeed effectively. It is the PMOs role to ensure that they are in place.

The second of these consists of formalizing the documents in the following chapters. It's always faster and easier to use a form. Creating a form involves energy and time that can be better used in other areas. Not only that but improving a form (or process) is always easier if you have a form that is used consistently. Tests are possible. Reviews are possible. Improvement is possible. If the form is new every time it's used then it is impossible to make it better. The skill and knowledge of the project manager creating the form will limit the quality. More importantly, so will the project manager's memory!

The other side of formalization is the process. (See, there was a reason I started from the back). Not only does this share the same quality issues but also it is inefficient to have the project manager design a new process every time a project is started. Picture for a moment a two-week one-person low-cost medium-value project performed by a junior programmer. Before starting, you'd have to have the project manager research the organization's human resource policies, document them and the design a process using them. Now imagine you'd need to do that for five or more processes. That one-week process would quickly become a two-month multi-person high-cost project. Or more likely, it would be refused or become a skunk project done without company oversight!

The common role of all PMOs is, therefore, to provide the process documentation which is the base for all projects. This is the subject of this chapter. Secondly, it is to provide the templates for the project information. That is the subject of the remaining chapters. After that, each organization needs to decide for itself which roles the PMO must fulfill.

Why Prepare Common Documents

If you examine the *PMBOK® Guide*, then you'll quickly find that the *PMBOK® Guide* expects three types of document to be produced by the project planning effort. Specifically it is looking for strategies, procedures and project documents. As I mentioned earlier, it is this combination that the rest of the world refers to as the project plan. For clarity's sake, I am referring to it as the project manual.

While the project documents produced are unique to each and every project, the procedures should be and often are, common for the vast majority of projects. The strategy documents typically share a mix of commonality and uniqueness.

By producing a document which, with minor customization, can apply to any project an organization achieves the following:

1. It reduces the time wasted by the project manager re-inventing the wheel in the form of project processes.
2. It provides a basis for continuous improvement through the use of forms and a defined process.
3. It reduces documentation development time through the use of boilerplate and forms.
4. It reduces the required size of documents through reference to pre-defined and standardized procedures and strategies.
5. It improves the quality of communications by providing a basis for common understanding.
6. It reduces the probability of conflict over the imposition of approval processes.

How To Document Procedures

In General

There are a million and one ways to document procedures. It seems like the only group more fascinated with developing alternative "best ways to do something" than business process analysts are programmers. Yes, I'm showing my IT biases here but I honestly believe that both groups have only two desires in life -- to create and to argue about their creations.

One group of business process analysts believes you should document using pictures. Another believes you should document using words. A third believes you should use both. A fourth believes you shouldn't document them at all! A fifth doesn't believe you should have procedures at all. But then again what would you expect from a profession that can't decide if they are business analysts, business systems analysts, systems analysts or business process analysts or quality analysts or ... Well, you get the idea.

In fact, the documentation needs to meet only four basic criteria:

1. Does it contain the important bits?
2. Is it read?
3. Is it understood?
4. Is it followed?

In fact, ultimately, only the first and last criteria matter!

So the truth of the matter is that the existence of the procedures matters. Their format doesn't. So feel free to use whatever format you prefer. Having said that, you do want the documentation to be simple and easily digested.

Documenting Projects In Particular

As you can tell from my previous comments, the processes associated with project management can be documented using the same methodology your organization prefers. However there are some pieces of process that are unique.

The first is an introduction to the process. This should not exceed three pages in length. It should however, cover the major points involved in the process. The project manager will use this document when communicating with people who are not commonly involved in the company's projects.

Frequently it is included as an appendix for the project manual.

The second is a one-paragraph template. This forms part of the project plan for most projects. In the legal profession, this is called "boilerplate". It should be simple, obvious, and focused on the important elements. To do this it should reference the extended documents in order to reduce the tendency of senior managers to skip over information. On the other hand, it should also allow the project manager to make most procedural adjustments without needing to do major rewriting. For example, most projects should use roughly the same project change management process. However, the amount the project manager can approve typically varies from project to project. If this is true for your projects, your boilerplate should include the ability to enter this amount.

The final difference is that most procedure documents only have one procedure per process. In order to create repetition, there is only one approved way to do things. This isn't necessarily true for projects. Instead, you may find that you need several possible procedures from which the project manager can chose the most appropriate. For example, the change management process for an Agile project will be completely different from that for a Waterfall project.

The Documentation You Need Before You Start Any Project

Project Change Procedures

There is no such thing as a project which begins knowing every little thing that must be done. There is no project which runs exactly according to plan. If there were, you wouldn't need the project manager to manage the project. You could just use a project planner.

Things change. Milestones are missed. Or they complete early. Better ways of working are determined. Presumptions are proven false.

All of these factors, result in the need to manage changes to the project. In the *PMBOK® Guide* parlance this process is sometimes called "change management" and sometimes called "integration". However you wish to name it, it represents control of your project. It keeps your project from morphing into another totally unexpected result. More importantly, it's there to prevent the source for 10% of the failures of projects (at least according to the Chaos report by the Standish Group).

Typically, the following elements are included in the project change procedures:

1. The various types of change request
2. How to submit a change request
3. How to determine the impact of the change request
4. How to approve a change request.
5. Who is authorized to approve a change request and at what level.
6. How to modify the project for change requests
7. How to close a change request
8. How to track a change request
9. How to decide to terminate a project due to a change.
10. How to close a project early (i.e. terminate it).

Of course, your list of elements may differ considerably from the above. Every organization has different rules and a process that best meets their culture, risk tolerance, desire for control and so on.

Procurement - Two Types

All projects involve procurement of something. It could include materials. It could include contractors. It could include employees. At the very least, it includes the assignment of the project team.

Projects are accomplished by directing and applying resources -- human and otherwise -- to a situation in a directed way in order to achieve a unique result. Those resources must be obtained somehow. Project managers call that process procurement.

There are two principle types of procurement.

- Materials

- People

At first glance, the difference appears to be related to what is acquired. However, in fact, it relates to the methods and difficulties involved in the procurement process.

Procurement Of Materials

The simplest form of procurement involves the purchase of materials. This includes both materials incorporated in the project and supplies used. However, it also includes items such as temporary office rental, audit services, marketing and so on.

The defining characteristic is that it involves the type of products and services a purchasing department would deal with. There are many different types of purchasing or procurement procedures possible. RFPs, RFQs, blanket purchase orders, are all part of the process. The process can involve the use of a common, corporate buying department or it may involve a project only buyer. Frequently there is a mix with certain items dealt with by a centralized service and other items dealt with by the project team.

Procurement Of Labor - Internal And External

Unlike a materials procurement process, the procurement of labor is typically considered to be a human resource issue. However, while it bears a close association with the human resource process and policies it is important enough to consider as a stand-alone process.

There are four main groups of labor you need to document:

- Internal

- External hiring

- External contracting with freelancers

- External contracts with service providers

Obtaining the appropriate individuals is a key success factor for any project. These individuals are your subject matter experts. Without the involvement of the right people, the project is doomed. After all, they are providing the expertise necessary to actually perform the project. The project manager's responsibility and skills need to focus on getting the players to work together. Choosing a project manager for his or her subject skills is a fool's game. All the technical issues together only account for slightly more failures (10.5%) than just one project process (change). In fact, individually they are the least important failure causes on the Chaos report (Other or miscellaneous accounts for 9.9%). As for the CITA study of 2007, they don't even rate an individual listing but get lumped in with the "other causes" total.

In some cases, a large portion of the team reports directly to the project manager. In other cases, a matrix type of arrangement is used and individuals are assigned temporarily. In any case, you will need to design a process specifically to work for your organization. The process must include the assignment of subject matter experts from both the primary service providing department and support experts which may come from any part of the organization.

Of course, not all skills are available within any organization. If the skills are not available within the company then it is necessary to obtain them from outside. This can mean retraining (which is under the Human Resources topic) but typically involves finding the skills outside.

In theory, projects are short-term, temporary endeavors. They shouldn't involve hiring new people. In practice, however, people are often hired for a project with the presumption that another project will appear to keep them busy. Typically, hiring procedures are company-wide and involve standardized practices.

A more theoretically supportable solution is to hire temporary workers with the correct skill set. One of the ways to do this involves the use of independent contractors (often referred to as freelancers). The organization contracts directly with the individual providing the service. Frequently, these individuals are hired through the same recruiters that supply full-time employees.

The other source of external expertise is the use of an external service provider. These companies hire their own people and then sign contracts with organizations to provide services. The service provider takes responsibility for the work package and provides an individual they believe is capable of performing the work. The process of engaging this type of organization often involves processes that are more reminiscent of purchasing than of hiring.

Each of these processes needs their own individual documentation. After all, their processes are different. Some projects will use only one source of people. However, many projects use a mix of the different choices. The documentation should provide for this mixture.

Hr Policies & Procedures

Of course, staffing a project is only the first step. Many other policies and procedures affect the relationship between the project manager, the team and the project staff. These policies and procedures need to be documented in the Human Resources Policies and Procedures documents.

The organization will normally have Human Resources policies and procedures documented for the whole company. In the case of a project, not all of these policies and procedures will apply. Equally, the nature of the project may require documentation of extended policies and procedures.

Risk Management Policies & Procedures

The last project document which should be created for all projects, is the risk management document. This needs to be a combination of procedures and strategies.

Not all changes occur because of increased knowledge. Some changes occur because of indeterminate events. Events which have a probability of occurring. This probability is called risk.

Risk events can have either a positive or negative effect. Actions need to be taken to enhance the risk (probability) of positive events and reduce the risk (probability) of negative events. In addition, costs are often incurred to reduce the effect of potential negative events. Finally, plans are put in place to take advantage of positive events and reduce the effect of negative events should they occur.

However, even the best plans cannot eliminate the effect of a negative risk event occurring. The effect of these risks need to be accounted for and managed.

Some of these effects can be absorbed and managed within the project. Effectively they expire on the completion of the project. They may occur or they may not. But the next project is a completely new game.

However, others need to be dealt with on a wider corporate basis. Often these are events where the cause is common to all or most projects. For example, one of the risk elements is the variance associated with estimation.

Sometimes estimations are high and sometimes they are low. If you are estimating effectively, on average the actual will be within 10%. However, for any particular project the estimation variation (also known as error) can be as high as 100%. In order to keep control of estimation variation, some form of overall management is required.

There are a number of different techniques used to deal with these issues. Project reserves for example, can be used to deal with those events that are manageable within the project. Corporate reserves can be used for those which aren't. Insurance is another method. In that case, the reserve is effectively moved outside the organization and combined with those of other organizations.

Typically, there is some form of approval or notification process which must be dealt with should a risk event occur. Often, this process is accompanied by a series of approval or notification levels. It is this process which needs to be documented.

In addition to the procedures, every organization has a tolerance for risk and risk exposure. This is often expressed in strategic terms and dealt with as a strategy for risk. The basic strategy (and tolerances) should also be documented.

You are now ready to start the project planning process.

Chapter 4

Getting Started — The Inputs

The Process Revisited

As I mentioned way back in Chapter 2, the basic process of initiating a project is fairly simple and straightforward -- in theory. Strategic and operational project requests are added to the portfolio. Projects are then selected from the portfolio in priority order and assigned to a project manager by the sponsor. The project manager and his team prepare a response detailing how they are going to accomplish the project. The sponsor then approves the response and the project begins. Along the way, the paperwork is prepared by the person or team performing the activity. It is then consolidated in the project manual.

In reality, what actually happens may be completely different. The most common variation is that the project manager and the team are forced to do the paperwork. Additionally, most sponsors will attempt to make this a one way information flow (i.e. "here's the work, now get lost"). Negotiation processes take up too much time since they are a cycle. Add to this the fact that the project plan is a combination of the four pieces of paperwork and it is almost a certainty that the purpose and process will be misunderstood. As a result, the separate elements become combined and quickly degrade into a political game of who is responsible and what will they accept.

This must be avoided at all costs. It is important to isolate the portfolio information, the assignment information, the project plan information and the approval to proceed. While little can be done about the executive's desire to offload work, separating the paperwork will help to ensure that the teams realize they are documenting the outputs of separate tasks.

What To Include In The Project Manual But Not The Project Plan

I have (arbitrarily) called the combination of the information a project manual. This is to differentiate it from the project planning (aka response) outputs (i.e. the project plan proper). In order to make a proper decision to proceed and to give proper direction to the project execution team, you need to also provide the "why" and the success criteria.

That means that the project manual needs to include three other items. Two of these are input to the planning process and are discussed in this chapter:

1. Portfolio Outputs
2. Charter Outputs

The third is the Approval document, which is discussed later.

Portfolio Outputs

In theory (and in practice) the portfolio process is the input to project initiation. Operational and strategic projects are requested. They are justified, ranked, and then selected for assignment based on a number of factors.

The main purpose of the information from the portfolio is to answer the questions "Why?", "When?" and "What?" Why are we doing this? What are we going to get from this? What are the criteria for success? This information helps to ensure that the project remains true to its original purpose.

Otherwise, well-meaning stakeholders will drive the result in a different direction.

One can expect the following pieces of information in each of the portfolio entries:

1. Basic Identifications
   1.a. A Portfolio Identifier.
   1.b. A Project Identifier.
2. Project Ownership
   2.a. Submitted By
   2.b. Responsibility Of:
3. Critical Resources.
4. Descriptive Information
   4.a. The Project Classification
   4.b. The Project Description.
   4.c. Success Definition
   4.d. Product(s) Description.
5. The Project Target Dates
6. Costs/Benefits & Financial Information
   6.a. Benefits Statement.
   6.b. Estimated Cost In $ (Target Budget)
   6.c. Estimated Benefit In $
   6.d. Return On Investment
   6.e. Rank or Priority

"Basic Identification" fields are fields that ensure uniqueness. All forms need to be unique and traceable. While the rest of the information is likely to be unique, these fields are specifically designed that way. Frequently, they are based on some variation of a sequential field. For this reason they are often referred to as (for example) Project Number. In fact, they often include both numeric and non-numeric values. They also tend to be pseudo-fields in that they are imposed on the meta-data structure rather than existing as part of the natural data. This is just a fancy way of saying they are selected or created by a designer to solve the problem of perfect uniqueness in an imperfect world. And the tendency of humans to not check before acting!

A "Portfolio Identifier" is a unique identifier used within the portfolio management system to identify a portfolio or group of related projects. Typically, it is unique for each strategic initiative. A common portfolio or group of portfolios is used for operational projects.

A "Project Identifier" is a unique identifier that is used throughout the life of a project from initiation to closure and beyond. A number of possible formats exist including sequentially numbered and multi-level sequential numbering (to handle sub-projects). In addition to being carried throughout the life of the project, it will be used on every document to provide a link for all documents describing the project. Occasionally, the project identifier incorporates the portfolio identifier in a hierarchical structure.

If a project does not belong to one person, then it is a project which will never be completed. The "Project Ownership" fields describe who is responsible for the success or failure of the project. The number of different types of ownership and their responsibilities for the project will vary from company to company. From the point of view of the assignment cycle, the "Project Ownership" fields answer the "Who?" question.

The "Submitted By" field is the name and identifier of the person who submitted the request. This is important in case any questions should arise.

The "Responsibility Of" field is the name and identifier of the person who owns or is primarily responsible for the project's success. This person typically appoints the sponsor.

One of the analyses that any project or strategic initiative should do is to determine what resources they absolutely must have. These "Critical Resources" can be people, materials, machinery or literally anything else.

However, they have one thing in common. If you don't have access to them, your project will be severely impacted to the negative. It might even fail.

What typically makes a project unique are the outputs and tasks that are going to be performed on it. Coding that information into the identifier is typically an inefficient and inelegant solution. The "Descriptive Information" fields are a better way to describe what is involved in a project that makes it unique. Typically, these are primarily text-based fields although some elements such as target date are numeric. From the point of view of the assignment cycle, the "Descriptive Information" fields answer the question "What?".

Every organization needs the ability to group projects together. This grouping could be by capital/expense, or it could be by strategic/operational or it could be by major task type (IT/financial/marketing etc.). That is the point of the "Project Classification" field. In simplest terms, it is whatever the company needs to create some form of logical organization around its projects. The bad news is that everyone is different in how they implement this need.

The "Project Description" field is frequently a dual or triple field consisting of a long description, title or short description and a very short description. In any case, you need to provide enough information to describe the purpose of the project.

The "Success Definition" in the charter needs to be a set of specific criteria. However, in the portfolio information all that is required is a basic description of what will constitute success. This is used to guide the sponsor and project manager in determining the criteria. It should always indicate which of the "triple constraints" (scope, time, cost or quality) is most important.

The "Product(s) Description" is a short description of what needs to be produced by the project. These outputs should be limited to those product(s) which justify the existence of the project. Outputs such as lessons learned which are produced by the project system do not need to be included.

Any project without "Project Target Dates" is doomed to never start (or finish). There will always be something more important. There are many variations of this information which can be included. For example, some organizations like to use "Latest Start Date" and "Duration" to provide the same information with some added political benefits. Some organizations will adjust this date based on the results of project planning. However, the preference is to keep this as the original targets. This allows easy identification of any Strategic Initiatives which are falling behind. In any case, the latest start date and the latest finish date for successful completion need to be described. From the point of view of the assignment cycle, this answers the question "When?".

The core of portfolio management largely consists of three major tasks: track outstanding projects, rank outstanding projects, and determine the value and cost of the outstanding projects. The last two, of course, are closely connected. The fields within the "Costs/Benefits & Financial Information" heading are associated with those two tasks. Of course, one could always ask why a project needs this information. As the project becomes more complex, more and more decisions will be made beyond the portfolio process. As we discovered from the Assignment cycle earlier, every decision needs to revolve around the "Why?" question. Otherwise, the result will head off in an unacceptable direction. From the point of view of the assignment cycle, these fields answer the question "Why?".

The "Benefits Statement" is really a discussion of the tangible and intangible benefits and costs of the project (or of the entire strategic initiative typically). It is the justification for the project. Generally, this consists of an extended discussion in the form of a report often called the Project Business Case.

The "Estimated Cost In $ (Target Budget)" is a single field numeric summary of the cost side of the benefits statement. It is used to direct the project manager so that the scope and plan is neither too rich nor too cheap. It is also used when selecting a project to ensure that company budgets are sufficient to begin and complete work on the project.

The "Estimated Benefit In $" is the opposite side (the benefit side) of the cost/benefit equation. Where the cost side is focused on tangible costs, the benefit side should also include allowances for intangibles. It helps the project manager and sponsor to determine when to recommend stopping a project. This helps to reduce runaway projects where the costs continue to mount until the actual "Return on Investment" (ROI) is below zero.

The "Return On Investment" is a calculated value (Benefit less the Cost all divided by the Cost). Its purpose is to ensure that the value received is high enough to justify the effort involved. It is also used when determining the relative priority of projects. Since there are always more projects than an organization can possibly do, it helps to ensure only the most valuable discretionary projects are performed. There are numerous variations on this field including internal rate of return, annualized rate of return as well as the vanilla version described here. Your organization may choose to use one or several of these variations.

While the information in the Benefits Statement forms the basis for placing the portfolio in a priority order, it has one issue. It's virtually impossible to sort into a useful form. Add the fact that part of the priority is not related to cost items and it becomes almost impossible to identify all the fields involved. To solve this issue most organizations provide some form of "Rank or Priority" system. The result of this decision process is entered into the "Rank or Priority" field. This allows for a simple sorting of the outstanding projects.

In the real world, a number of other fields exist within the portfolio documents. For example, "status" is pretty well universal. However, since the portfolio is only supposed to hold projects awaiting assignment, and the only projects I care about are those in the initiation phase (meaning now changing from awaiting to active); I really don't care about that field. Similarly, other fields may exist due to organization desires or needs.

Many of these relate to creating a dashboard of information for the executive. For example, "Estimated Completion Date" and "Spending to Date" are frequently found on the record. Care should be taken -- especially with these dashboard data elements -- not to include information which is actually generated as part of the project plan. This frequently happens when the portfolio, active and completed to date projects are combined for executive reporting.

One of the other situations that may exist is related to the use and issuance of project numbers. Typically, portfolio management doesn't appear until project management has been in place for some time. The established procedure is therefore to assign project numbers when the project is initiated. When portfolio management is introduced, project numbers should be assigned when the project is defined (i.e. during the portfolio process). However, some organizations will use a sub-portfolio number to uniquely identify the project during its portfolio lifetime in order to avoid changing the existing process.

Project Charter

The project charter is probably the most misunderstood document in the whole project cycle (not just initiation -- the whole thing). A large part of this misunderstanding has to do with who actually fills in the form. While the sponsor (or their boss) should be filling in the form, typically it is left up to the project manager to do. Making matters worse, the project manager then brings in the project team to help develop the information. At which point it suddenly gets all confused with the response (i.e. project plan).

In fact, the project charter's sole purpose is to document the assignment of the project manager and the team.

The project charter should not include the opinions and thoughts from the project team. Instead, it is the first half of a contract between the sponsor and the project manager (and the team). It should contain the opinions of the sponsor so that the original request can be documented. Effectively, it is the standard against which the project plan and the project as a whole, is measured.

The charter only needs to contain five pieces of information:

1. The Project Identifier
2. The Purpose Statement
3. The Participants:
   3.a. The Owner of the Project
   3.b. The Sponsor of the Project
   3.c. The Project Manager
   3.d. Pre-assigned Project Team Members
4. The Objectives of the Project

5. Limits of Authority

The "Project Identifier" field is the same project identifier that is used throughout the whole project. Frequently it includes the "Portfolio Identifier" within it. I've already discussed this field so I'm not going to repeat the information.

The "Purpose Statement" is a simple, single sentence in three parts. It answers the questions, "What?", "How Much?" and "When?". The format of the purpose statement follows a set format: "To <do what> at a cost of <cost> by <target date>". For example, the purpose statement for this book read, "To write a book about Documenting Projects at a cost of one week's work by 2011.10.15".

The "Participants" fields answer the question of "Who?" is involved. More specifically, they answer the questions of responsibility and availability. How much information is included for each of these fields depends on the organization. In some cases, name and employee number are needed. In other cases, only name. In still others, name and extension.

I've already discussed the concept of the "Owner" of the project. So I'm not going to repeat myself. I do want to explain myself however. Arguably, including the owner is a duplication of information. After all, it's included in the portfolio outputs. However, frequently the owner of the project changes between the requesting of the project and the actual assignment. It makes sense then to recapture the information at the start of the project.

The second participant we need to identify is the "Sponsor". Although I've mentioned the role several times, I haven't really explained who the sponsor is and their role in the project. The sponsor is the executive who has been given ultimate responsibility for the project's success. This can be the owner, but is often a subordinate of the owner. Their role is to support the project manager, coordinate and market the project with other executives, and to resolve issues the project manager does not have the authority to resolve. The sponsor, for example, approves scope changes or coordinates the submission and management of changes with the supervising board.

The "Project Manager" field identifies the individual who is tasked with managing the project.

Finally, the "Pre-assigned Team Members" lists the project team members assigned to assist with the project planning. While they are usually the actual team for co-

coordinating efforts, they are more likely to be department managers rather that the individuals actually performing the work. Of course, each company is different and the resulting project reporting-structure is often confused and convoluted.

One of the worst things you can do to a subordinate is to give them a job and then not tell them what they have to do to be successful. The "Objectives of the Project" expands on the "Success Definition" from the portfolio. All of the objectives should be specific, measurable, attainable, relevant and timely (SMART). However, in addition, they should be stated in a yes/no manner. They should also indicate how they are to be measured. For example, the criteria "Easy to use" is meaningless in this context. On the other hand, the criteria "Achieves a rating of 4 out of 5 from a survey of users questioning ease of use" is useful for our purposes because it includes a way of measuring the result. When the project is completed, the project manager should be able to list the criteria, answer the question and be able to prove exactly how successful they were in achieving those criteria.

It can be argued that the "Limits of Authority" field doesn't really belong on the charter. Until the sponsor approves the project plan, the project manager is only responsible for producing the project plan. However, the limits of the project manager's authority may affect the project strategy. Some discussion and recording of the limits should occur prior to approval.

In addition, to the above fields there are a number of fields included in most project charter packages to help further refine the assignment. While they aren't really part of the charter, it makes sense to capture the information provided by the sponsor.

For example, the scope is not really necessary. The purpose statement performs that purpose. As does the request information from the portfolio. However, it is common to include a high-level scope statement expanding on the purpose and providing guidance as to what will be and what won't be included in the project.

Similarly, requirements are not really appropriate at this point. However, high-level requirements are often included to capture the knowledge of the sponsor.

Finally, it is common to identify key stakeholders. These are the individuals the sponsor wishes the project manager to target usually for their contribution.

What Do We Have?

At this point, the project manager (and his or her team) have been asked to prepare a plan to address the project.

The project manual will include the following:

1. A title page
2. Appendices:
   2.a. Portfolio Detail Record (usually called a project request form)
   2.b. Portfolio Business Case (the justification)
   2.c. Project Charter (this is sometimes used as the title section)
   2.d. One-page descriptions of the standard project processes.

We now have the information needed to respond to the assignment. We can go on to creating our response to the assignment -- better known as the project plan.

Chapter 5

The Response

Whenever I discuss the purpose of project management, I remember two quotes. The first is the Boy Scout motto "Be Prepared". The second, "No plan survives first contact with the enemy", is by Helmuth Karl Bernhard Graf von Moltke. The von Moltke the Elder quote in particular has been misused many times. (Hey, the German actually translates as "No plan of operations extends with certainty beyond the first encounter with the enemy's main strength" so what would you expect?)

What is the purpose of a project plan?

While it is certainly true that von Moltke the Elder was correct, the value of planning lies in the Scout motto. The purpose of planning is to predict the future in order to avoid losing -- in other words, to know when to cut and run. In the business world, that translates as avoiding bad decisions.

The Planning Process

The *PMBOK® Guide* breaks the planning process down into one phase, nine knowledge areas, five process groups and forty-two processes. The initiation phase requires the following knowledge areas:

1. Project Integration Management
2. Project Scope Management
3. Project Time Management
4. Project Cost Management
5. Project Quality Management
6. Project Human Resources Management
7. Project Communications Management
8. Project Risk Management
9. Project Procurement Management

I'm not going to go into details about the forty-two tasks but, as you can see from the list, the *PMBOK® Guide* view is very complex.

In the real world outside of the PMP® exam, you can reorganize all of this complexity to focus on the task at hand.

One can visualize the project planning view as five streams of plans and the processes to support those streams.

1. Stakeholders
2. Requirements
3. Risks
4. Scheduling
5. Costing

This makes for a much simpler set of documentation without losing any of the details.

So why can I make this simplification in the real world?

In the *PMBOK® Guide* world, there are two assumptions that flavor the standard. The first is that one needs to include the whole project management process. The second is that time (also sequence) does not exist. As a result, the *PMBOK® Guide* separates the initiation and planning processes in order to ensure the change management sub-system includes the same steps as the original planning phase. As a result, a number of additional tasks appear. These tasks allow planning to occur during the execution of a project.

Both of these are presumptions made to assist in understanding concepts. In the real world, it is perfectly acceptable to consider the assignment of a task separate from the performance of the task. And it is perfectly acceptable to assign both timing and sequencing to activities. In fact, in this particular case, it is virtually required to do so. If one intends to be successful, it is mandatory to prepare a plan before performing the project. Moreover, a project team doesn't necessarily want to implement change management while negotiating the project.

I, however, do not operate under the limitation of trying to document the whole process of project management. Nor do I need to ignore time and sequencing. At least for this book.

Start by adding time and sequence. Then, view the initial planning process separately from revision during the execution (i.e. the change process). The result is that I am able to simplify much of what I am describing. Similarly, by ignoring the knowledge areas and focusing on information streams I am able to simplify our view of the processes.

There is one caveat. The addition of sequence applies only to the overall process. Within planning, each stream can affect other streams. The addition of quality requirements identifies new risks; new risks identify new tasks; new tasks identify new stakeholders. The wave of knowledge doesn't just erupt from the execution phase. Every examination creates its own wave. Planning illuminates the future. As I mentioned earlier, that's what planning is all about. Predicting the future. Making choices in order to illuminate further choices.

The Structure Of The Project Plan

Unfortunately, the typical management response is "Plans -- we don't need no stinkin' plans!" (Yes, I've been watching too much Mel Brooks and John Huston. I've never read B. Traven, so I'll apologize to him). In fact, while a certain amount of that emotion focuses on planning most of it is really directed at the costs of planning. It is always incumbent on the project manager to ensure that the planning document is never longer than it needs to be (and that it's never longer than management will accept).

When determining your own documentation, always keep in mind the "Just Enough" principle. And that you may need to use different layers to provide your project management stakeholders with "just enough" information. By the way, that middle word is important. I'm not talking about the project stakeholders. I'm talking about that subset who either manages the project, or is managed by the project.

In this documentation, I am using a three-layer structure. Think medium to large organizations (but not mega-corps), where your time is less important than the executive's time. This might be appropriate where the project management structure consists of:

- Executive (perhaps the CEO)

- Sponsor

- Project Manager

- Project Team

Depending on your own organization's structure and needs, you may need more layers or less. In my consulting life, I have worked with methodologies that specified four or more layers. Yet others specified only one. However, I believe this structure is appropriate in far more situations.

The basic structure of the project plan -- and the project manual for that matter -- is an executive report. With an executive report, you place the details in appendices and various levels of detail within the report itself. For our purposes this means the report consists of:

- An Executive Summary

- The main report

- Appendices

The first layer is the executive report. When writing the executive summary you should target to present your summary in one paragraph. Of course, reality raises its not-so-pretty head and you may need to make it a very long paragraph. Or two or three. However, keep in mind that your target is five points only:

1. What you're going to do
2. How much it will cost
3. When you're going to do it
4. Why you're doing it
5. Who will be involved

Any other information is extra fluff. Unfortunately, you will find living in the real world (and dealing with real people) demands some of that fluff. For example, giving a short sentence or two on the strategy is typically a very good thing. As is a sentence or two on major project risks. In fact, a sentence or two on each of the project plan streams described in the rest of this book is wise.

Your job in the executive summary is three-fold. You need to give the general reader enough of an introduction to the project to understand the rest of what they are reading. You need to provide enough information for the executive to believe you have everything well in hand. And finally, you need to provide as little information as possible so that those suffering from ADHD will actually read the summary at least.

The second layer or main body of the report is why PMI believes the project plan is strategy only, while the rest of the world believes it is the schedule. This layer is for the executive who wants and needs more information. The sponsor is a good example. It should consist of a short document (five to nine pages long). The project manager (okay, his team) should discuss each of the questions in roughly a paragraph. In fact, the project manager should include a one-paragraph summary of each of the artifacts or documents developed by the planning process. This includes the boilerplate developed for the standard strategies (see Chapter 3).

A simple summary is sufficient for the sponsor and any detail-oriented executives. However, the project manager and the people doing the work will need much more detail. This detail is hidden in the appendices where it is available for those with a need for it. However, it is separated from the core project information for those who do not require details.

What To Include In The Project Plan

I know I'm turning this into a broken record, but every organization has its own definition of what the main Project Plan needs to include. However, at a bare minimum it needs to include the following:

1. The Strategic Discussions
   1.a. Discussion of the Overall Project Strategy
   1.b. Specific Strategic & Process Variation Discussions
      1.b.i. How to handle project changes
      1.b.ii. How to handle materials procurements
      1.b.iii. How to handle personnel procurements
      1.b.iv. Human Resource variations and strategy
      1.b.v. How to handle project risk
2. The Project Planning Outputs (The Planning Streams)

2.a. The Stakeholder Communications stream

2.b. The Requirements Stream

2.c. The Risks Stream

2.d. The Scheduling Stream

2.e. The Cost Management Stream

Now that I've placed everything in context, let's look at the outputs from each of the streams in detail.

Chapter 6

The Stakeholder /Communications Stream

No project exists in a vacuum. All projects involve people. Some of those people are on the project team. Some of those people manage the project team. Some of those people work for the project team. Some of those people are related to the project team. Some of those people use the products of the project. Some of those people are affected by the project.

All of those people are stakeholders.

One can argue that the sole reason a project exists is for the stakeholders. After all, they use the product, are affected by the product or profit from the product. They also decide the requirements for the project. Ultimately, they will determine the success or failure of the project.

Is it any wonder that a project needs to consider them in the planning?

Taking an overall view, the Stakeholder/ Communications stream provides the plans for determining the communications requirements of the project. There are two major types of communications involved. The first is project status and similar reports. The second is one of the defining characteristics of the Holistic Philosophy. The second type of communication concerns the changes imposed by the project and the reaction of the Stakeholders to the project.

Taking a more detailed view, the Stakeholder/ Communications stream consists of three major processes:

1. Identification of the Stakeholders
2. Stakeholder Impact Analysis
3. Communications Analysis

The Stakeholders

It always helps to know to whom you are talking.

It doesn't matter whether you are discussing writing a book, selling a product, giving a speech or planning a project. You need to understand your audience. But first, you need to know who they are.

That's the purpose of this process. To identify with whom you need to communicate. Why? So you can communicate with them about the things that they care about, in the way that they want to communicate.

During your investigation, you are going to going to do more than just identify the stakeholders. You are also going to identify certain facts about them. All of these facts need to be entered in a simple form of CRM. CRM is a fancy name for a contacts, or name and address system. (It actually stands for Customer Relationship Management.)

Everyone and every CRM system has their opinion of what should be included. However, as a minimum, this list of your stakeholders should include the following information:

1. Stakeholder Identification
   1.a. Stakeholder Id.
   1.b. Name
2. Contact Information
   2.a. Phone Number
   2.b. Fax
   2.c. Email
   2.d. Address
3. Group
4. Information Needed
   4.a. Information Description
   4.b. Preferred Contact Method
   4.c. Preferred Contact Frequency

All of the records in a project need to be unique. You need to be able to identify and reference the specific instance that creates information. The list of stakeholders is no different. You need some form of unique identification -- "The Stakeholder Identification".

This unique field needs to contain at minimum two fields.

The first is a unique pointer. Sometimes people call it a "Stakeholder Id.". Sometimes it is a Stakeholder Number. Sometimes it is a Stakeholder Id. Number. And sometimes it is something else entirely. The key characteristic is that it is artificial (i.e. created by someone) and it is unique.

This artificial identifier exists because the real world identifier is not unique. I'm referring, of course, to the "Name". Stakeholders are people. People have names. People identify themselves by their names. Unfortunately, people often share the same name. So to meet real world beliefs and actually build in uniqueness, It is necessary to keep both the name and an artificial key.

There is also a need to keep track of "Contact Information" for this individual. After all, that's the point of this whole stream. We need to communicate or contact the people with information about the project. There is some flexibility in the contact information you will need to track.

In order to send mail and printed information, you must maintain their "Address". Of course, the definition of address can vary. Internally it may be an office, or a maildrop or a department. Externally, it can be a street number, street and city. Or it can be a post office box. Or it can be all of those.

Some people like to be emailed rather than receive physical mail. After all, email can be filed much easier than you can physical mail. Plus it takes up less space. To be able to email your stakeholders you need to maintain their "Email Address". In fact, you may need to maintain multiple email addresses.

The third favored method of contact is the phone. Phone calls have a number of advantages over any other method. They allow someone to communicate with both inflection and words. They allow you to receive feedback. And they allow you to modify your message based on that feedback. However, they do need you to maintain the "Phone Number". This may include the extension or it may be limited to the extension. You may also find that you need multiple phone numbers. It's quite common to maintain an office number, home number and cell number.

The most common variation is the "Fax Number". While other variations are simply targets for phone calls, fax is a separate type of communications. It is used to send light text-based information. Arguably, fax is an obsolete technology. However, many stakeholders continue to use it. Some even demand its use for certain types of communications.

There are a number of alternative, cutting-edge forms of contact. However, most of them are "pull" communications. In other words, a message is placed in a central location where it is accessed when and if an individual is interested. Facebook, the web and Twitter are all examples of this type of communication. This is especially true for the social media. The organization needs to identify which of these it will use. These "pull" communications do not need to track information in order to create a connection. "Push" communications however, need to have an address of some type.

In the real world, the "Group" field has a number of names. It can be called a type, a group, or a class, just to name a few. Stakeholders naturally separate into groups which share common characteristics. For example, you might have the public, A/R clerks, Finance management and project management as groups. Each project will have its own list of groups. Each organization will have its own name for groups. But all projects need to group stakeholders together in order to manage them.

The "Information Needed" fields describe the stakeholder's information needs. For example, the stakeholder may need monthly progress reports or periodic warnings of project changes. Three pieces of data combine to make this information.

The first is an "Information Description". This is simply a text description of the types of information that the Stakeholder needs to see. For example, progress reports or change notices.

The second element you need to capture is the "Preferred Contact Method". This is one of the choices which you identified earlier (under Contact Information). Stakeholders often require force-fed information or they may have a preference for a particular type of self-serve information.

Finally, you need to capture how often the Stakeholder wishes to receive the information. This is the "Preferred Contact Frequency". For example, they may wish to receive the information as it occurs or have it consolidated to a weekly or monthly report.

Arguably the "Group" and "Information Needed" fields are managed during the Communications Analysis phase and therefore don't belong at this stage. But then again, the "Information Needed" fields are usually related to the "Group" rather than the individual Stakeholder. However, the information is typically identified when identifying the Stakeholders. So I've included it at this stage -- even if it will be finalized later.

Stakeholder Impact Analysis

The term "Impact Analysis" is really a meaningless term. In order to properly define any impact analysis you need a subject and an object. For example, you can analyze the impact of revisions on the project plan. You can analyze the impact of new team members on the team. You could even analyze the effect of moonlight marigolds on the project and call it an impact analysis. All of them qualify as impact analysis.

The only phrase with less meaning is change management. Change management's meaning changes with every user. To a programmer, change management is what project managers call configuration management. To a human resources professional, change management is the management of people's reactions to change. To a project manager, it is the management of the impact on the project from new knowledge and revisions.

Arguably, of those three only the last is really change management. Why? Because it is the only one that is actually managing the changes. The rest all manage the effect from a change.

However, to keep the concepts straight I am going to avoid the term "change management" altogether. We've already run into the project manager's view of change management. For that I have used the term "Project Change Procedures".

I have, in the past, used the term "reaction management" to describe the reality behind what human resources and psychologists call change management. After all, that's what you are really managing -- the individual's reaction to change. You aren't managing the change itself. However, in this case I'm going to use the term "Stakeholder Impact Analysis". Why? Because we are analyzing the impact on the Stakeholder of the project.

Whatever term you use, this is one of the keys to holistic project management. To be holistic you need to consider all the elements that go into a project and making it successful. In the past, project managers have ignored the effect of their projects on the stakeholders. After all, the project is going to go ahead in any case, isn't it? And hopefully, someone took into account the stakeholders when the decision was made.

Ignoring the reaction of people to the project has resulted in surprise failures when the stakeholders have rebelled. Although the project itself was successful, no one ended up using the product. In other cases, rampant changes to the scope and requirements caused the project itself to fail.

When I was less old and less foolish with intent, I led a project which successfully failed. It was a simple project. Help the stock receiver enter what they receive by having the buyers pre-enter what will be received. I actually went beyond and gave the buyers the chance to enter a purchase order. That way, they received a benefit from entering the information and the receiver got his information entered by someone else. Simple. Easy. No big deal.

Of course, it failed. The buyers refused to enter the information and the receiver was constantly complaining that the product was received before the purchase order had been cut.

So what happened? Why did it fail?

My mistake had been to ignore the effect on the buyers of the change. As it turned out, the buyers called the manufacturer who decided what was being purchased and how much was needed. The effect on the buyers of this minor change was to prove that they weren't doing anything useful. So they rebelled and allowed the purchase orders to back up.

The prevention of situations similar to my story is the whole point of this process. The purpose of this process is to identify how the stakeholder will react, and then determine a strategy to turn that reaction into a positive result. In that way, the project manager can prevent surprises.

Like most analyses, the majority of the work occurs by thinking about existing information. What information is generated tends to be in the form of text. In this case, you will be identifying reactions and a strategy to refocus that reaction to a more positive result. In this case you do need to track some information, specifically you need to record:

1. Group or Name
2. Impact (by the project)
3. Priority/Extent/Importance
4. Expected Reaction
5. Alternatives
6. Strategy

Each of the reaction strategies needs be focused on one or more groups of individuals or directly on specific individuals. You will therefore need to identify your strategy with a specific "Group or Name". Although I have combined both fields, you may find that you need to provide separate identifiers. In that case, while you will need one of the identifiers completed, the other should have a null value (meaning it doesn't exist).

Once you've identified who we are discussing, you need to identify how they are being affected by the project. This is the purpose behind recording the "Impact" by the project. Frequently, this is a description field. However, the ability to group types of impacts together is a very useful tool as projects increase in complexity.

Of course it helps to know how badly the individuals will be impacted by the project. Often the strength of the reaction is proportional to how much the individual is affected. Where many analyses fail is in not recognizing that psychological and emotional impact trumps physical impact. In any case, you need to track some form of rating of the strength of the impact in the "Priority/Extent/Importance" field.

Of course, different people will react differently to the changes. Not all of these reactions will be negative. Part of the analysis process is to identify how the individual is expected to react in order to prepare a strategy to control the reaction. This information is kept in the "Expected Reaction" description.

Of course, people being people, it is hard to predict how they will react. Often there are a number of possible reactions. It is helpful to record those which are less likely than the expected reaction in the "Alternatives" field.

Once you have determined what the reaction will be and why it is possible to determine a desired outcome and the strategy to refocus the individual towards that result. Most of the time this strategy will focus on some form of communications and project involvement. In any case, the strategy is described in the "Strategy" field.

Communications Analysis

At this point you now have a list of the stakeholders, their desire for information and the effect of the project on them. You also have a strategy for refocusing that effect. It is now time to turn those into a set of communications tasks. These pieces of information and the details of their communication form your communications plan.

Obtaining the information, repurposing the information and then distributing the information will result in a draw on the resources of the project. If you don't identify the communications needs you will find that needed communications will not occur. And worse, the time spent to generate the communications will not appear in the budget for the project.

Many organizations have some form of standard for the communications that they expect to see generated during the execution phase of a project. However, the project manager should still analyze the stakeholders' needs. This is especially true with regards to the Stakeholder Impact Analysis and the communications needs it identifies. In any case, some form of list of the communications needs should be developed. This will include at a minimum:

1. Type of Communication
2. Frequency
3. Communication Method
4. Description
5. Information Contained
6. Responsibility
7. Recipient(s)/Stakeholder(s)

It is very difficult to sort a text-based description. Doing so tends to give nonsensical results. However, by using a one or two word summary it is possible to sort similar communications together. The "Type of Communications" field can also be considered part of the complex key that identifies this communication.

The "Frequency" is the second of the three fields that make up the complex key. Some stakeholders will want to see their information on a weekly basis. Others on a biweekly basis. Still others on a monthly basis. Not all of which will be provided of course. However, the "Frequency" allows for different timings of the communications.

The final field is the "Communication Method". Some stakeholders will be receiving the information by email. Others in person. Still others by a phone call. This field allows the project manager to specify the media to use.

While it is theoretically possible to identify all the characteristics of all communications it is much easier to simply define a text description field. After all, no matter how good the analyst, there will always be new characteristics appearing. The "Description" field assists the reader to understand the nature of the communication.

While it can be argued that the "Description" field can provide all of the required information, the use of a separate "Information Contained" field allows the project manager to be specific in what type of information is communicated.

Like most tasks unless one person is responsible for the creation and transmission of the information it will not occur. The person identified in the "Responsibility" field may not be the person actually creating the information. However, they are the individual responsible for it being created and distributed.

The final piece of information that is required is the "Recipient(s)/Stakeholder(s)". Project management -- especially holistic project management -- is not about creating communications for the sake of paperwork. A communication needs both a creator (the person with the "Responsibility") and a receiver (the "Recipient(s)/Stakeholder(s)").

Chapter 7

The Requirements Stream

Many years ago I wanted to write fiction. So I joined a local writers group. This was a group of people of varying skill and experience who had one characteristic in common. We all loved to write.

I remember two individuals in particular. One was a published novelist who had recently made the leap to creating pulp fiction full time. The other was a former schoolteacher. Now retired, she wanted to create a great romance novel.

Our weekly meetings were peppered with their arguments. "Always write to a plan.", one would argue. "Great art just appears.", the other would reply. "Great art is free.", would follow "Great art starts with well-executed craft." And so the argument would bounce back and forth. "A book must be planned fully.", was thrown against the wall of "I want my book to go where it wants to go."

When I left construction to work in what was then termed "Computers" or "MIS", I found the same argument had been repeated. By the time I joined the industry the "craft" argument had surpassed the "art" argument. I found that information systems (as they were later known) had borrowed a page from construction. No project could begin until the requirements had been formalized, rubber stamped, approved, disproved, and reapproved. Oh, and the solution had to be designed first. The "design-as-you-go" school had faded under a demand for quality software that didn't collapse under the weight of changes.

Of course, in the real world the rule was closer to "Fix foot, shoot, aim, fix foot again, wonder why head hurts".

Many years later the argument is still going on. Now, the create-on-the-fly position is held by the Agile folks. And it is the Waterfall folks who are on the defensive. Not just in IT but in many other industries as well.

Whichever side of the argument you come down on, a project needs to have a handle on what it is building. It needs to research and understand the product. It needs to research and understand why the product needs to exist. And it needs to do this at least in part before planning the product in order to have an understanding of the tasks necessary to create that product.

Project managers call that process either Requirements Management or Scope Management.

The requirements stream consists of the results of the research, the limitations on the requirements imposed by management and the quality requirements identified during the research. I call the first "Requirements", the second "Scope" and the latter "Quality".

The Requirements

No matter which side of the Agile/Waterfall debate you find yourself on there is a need to determine the requirements of the product being developed. In construction it could be the number of floors to the building or the number of bedrooms. In software it could be the number of orders or the number of fields on a data entry screen.

These requirements are determined by interviewing a cross section of stakeholders and a number of key stakeholders. Typically the interviews and documentation are conducted by specialists. These specialist SMEs are particularly trained to identify requirements and document the needs in a format that is most appropriate to the subject. For example, business analysts, business systems analysts and business process analysts are some of the SMEs that research and document information systems' needs. Architects and engineers research and document the requirements for a construction project. And so on.

Each of these disciplines has developed their own form of documentation. However, for all of them, there are two sets of documentation that are required.

The first is detailed and will be in the format that is most appropriate to the subject of the project. This may in fact, be a set of documents of varying levels of detail. For example, an architectural drawing and a parts list is one form of detailed requirements.

The second set of documents is simply a list of the requirements which is sometimes referred to as a log. As a minimum it must contain:

1. Requirements Id.
2. Stakeholder Who Requested
3. Who Investigated
4. When Submitted
5. When Required
6. Description
7. Impact on Project
8. Test/Compliance Verification
9. Status

One of the most common elements of requirements management is the ability to track functions within the product back to the requirements that identified the need for that function. A numeric or modified numeric field using letters for a sequence identifier often provides for this need for a cross-reference to the requirement, and for uniqueness. I am calling this the "Requirements Id.". The nature of this field will vary from organization to organization.

No matter how well the analyst documents the requirement, there are always questions. Conflicting requirements, poorly understood requirements, or a lack of detail are all sources of these questions. It is important therefore to identify the "Stakeholder Who Requested" the requirement. This can be a name or link to the Stakeholder information (the Stakeholder Id.).

For the same reason it is important to identify who documented the requirement. Often a weakness in communication is at the root of questions. The analyst can frequently answer these types of questions without having to discuss the situation with the stakeholder. It is therefore important to identify the analyst through the "Who Investigated" field.

One of the unfortunate realities is that requirements change over time. Sometimes it is the result of actual changing conditions. Sometimes it is the result of time to think and different decisions. As a result it is always important to record "When Submitted" and to be prepared to revisit older requirements.

On the other hand, delivery is required, for certain requirements, by a specific date. This is quite prevalent when dealing with compliance issues. In other cases the requirement has an expiry date. If not delivered by that date the requirement is no longer valid. This date is maintained in the "When Required" field.

While the details for the requirement are maintained in a separate document, it helps if a summary can be maintained in the list or log. That summary is stored in the "Description" field.

Of course, all requirements have a cost. This cost can appear as a simple dollar figure. More likely, however, the cost will appear in terms of an "Impact on Project". This description field allows one to measure the return on investment of the requirement and therefore prioritize the requirements.

One issue that all requirements face is how to prove that they were properly delivered. The "Test/Compliance Verification" field describes how the project manager can decide and prove that the requirement has been delivered as requested.

It would be nice if every possible requirement could be accomplished immediately. Unfortunately, that's just not possible. There is always a limit to the amount of work possible in a given period. By identifying which requirements are being including in the current phase, which were completed previously and which are being delayed to a future phase, it is possible to account for all requirements without having to actually do them all immediately. That is the point of the "Status" field.

Scope

Projects fail for many reasons. Requirements and people skills are the two major reasons for failure. More specifically, the requirements issues are that either the requirements were not identified up front or else the project ran away with the requirements. Poor scope management is one of the major causes of project failure.

Scope is essentially the management control of high-level requirements. It describes both what will be delivered and what won't be delivered as part of the project. Requirements can become quite detailed. However, the scope is always dealing with broad-brush elements.

In the holistic philosophy, the requirements identify what the users and stakeholders in general want from the system. The scope, on the other hand, describes what management believes is the extent of the project.

Scope gives the project manager direction when accepting a requirement. The requirement can be within the scope of the project. This implies that it needs to be done. Or it can be outside the scope of the project. This implies that management needs to approve both it and the extra costs.

This allows management to retain control on what the project is trying to accomplish and therefore allows it to retain control of the costs involved.

A typical scope statement includes three documents. We've already discussed the first document. It is the "Project Changes" process. This document discusses the standard method of managing the scope statement.

The second is a strategy document detailing the changes to the pre-defined scope management process. This includes the addition of variable information such as approval levels. This document is generally a text template or boilerplate.

The third document that is produced is the Scope Statement itself. This document is typically also text based. Usually it includes the following information:

1. Summary
2. Specific Includes (boundary)
3. Specific Excludes (boundary)
4. Project Deliverables
5. Project Constraints
6. Project Assumptions/Presumptions

Management tends to describe scope in very generic terms. Often this description is more indicative of the intent than the specific boundaries. The "Summary" contains this description.

Traditionally, scope consists of a generic description plus a number of specific instances that provide a description of the boundary of the scope. Items specifically inside the scope (i.e. included in the project) are listed in the "Specific Includes (boundary)" field.

Similarly, part of the description includes those items which are specifically determined to be outside of the scope. Those items are listed in the "Specific Excludes (boundary)" field.

An important part of the scope is, of course, the "Project Deliverables". After all, that is what the project is all about. The "Project Deliverables" field is used to list the product and services of the project.

Projects take place in the real world. They do not have access to unlimited resources. They operate in an environment of real and perceived "Project Constraints". This field is used to identify any element in the environment which may limit the project.

One of those unlimited resources that project managers dream of having access to is perfect knowledge. Unfortunately, project managers must operate in an environment of unknowns. They must make logical interpretations (in other words guesses). Typically, these involve assumptions if possible, but far more often presumptions. What's the difference? An assumption is proven and therefore true. A presumption has yet to be proven. Not knowing the difference is what gets project managers in trouble. In any case, the "Project Assumptions/Presumptions" field is for the project manager to list the assumptions or presumptions upon which the project depends.

Quality

One of the skills that every project manager should have is the ability to work as a quality assurance analyst. Perhaps not full time, however a basic understanding is mandatory.

Quality appears in a project both in the product and in the project management process itself. As management has learned in the past sixty years, it is always cheaper and easier to build quality into the process. Adding it in afterwards is always more expensive and less effective.

During the requirements phase business analysts typically receive hints regarding the level of quality required. Or more frequently solicit them. Unfortunately, these hints are seldom as definitive as they need to be. Not all projects are as lucky in this respect as construction, where the standard is predefined and a matter of law. So the project manager and the project team typically need to identify the quality standard that will be used.

They also need to build tasks into the process in order to ensure that the project achieves the desired level of quality.

Typically the quality process will produce two documents. The first is a statement of how the project is going to meet the quality standards (and in general what standard). This is the quality strategy.

The second document is a more detailed list of the quality requirements. This may include such things as when quality control tests will occur. Who will provide the testing? What standards will be met? What quality control tests will be used? And so on. In general you should create a list with the following information for each requirement:

1. Quality Requirement Id.
2. Description
3. Metric/Standard/Baseline
4. How to Achieve
5. How to Prove

As with other requirements, it is important to be able to connect the dots. You need to be able to reference a unique Quality Requirement and prove that it was satisfied. The "Quality Requirement Id." provides the unique identifier for each requirement. This can be just about anything but typically, it is a numeric key.

Every organization and every type of project the organization does will have a different configuration of information regarding the quality requirements. The easiest solution to this is to use a textual "Description" field to hold the quality requirement information.

The first mandatory element is the "Metric/Standard/Baseline". Every quality requirement has a standard that it needs to meet. This standard is sometimes called a metric or baseline. In any case, every requirement needs to describe the standard being met.

The second mandatory element that every organization needs is a field to indicate "How to Achieve" the quality requirement. This can be as simple as a single test or as complex as a strategy for added tasks in the schedule.

Of course, no requirement can be relied on unless it can be proven to be achieved. The "How to Prove" field allows the project manager and team to describe how the project will prove that the requirement was met.

Chapter 8

The Risk Stream

What is the difference between an entrepreneur and a working stiff?

It's certainly not intelligence. And it's not willingness to work. Or unwillingness. It's not in their training or vocation. There's an old saying that an entrepreneur is a person who was unlucky enough to lose his job, and lucky enough to create a new one. So it's not luck.

The answer lies in their attitude towards risk.

Now, I come from a long line of entrepreneurs. I like to say that I learned to be an entrepreneur at my Great-Grandfather's knee. In fact, my Grandfather, Father and

Uncles all had a hand in my training. As far back as I can trace the Ford family we've been entrepreneurs.

I'm comfortable with risk.

A few years back I learned a very important lesson regarding risk management. I was working as a systems analyst with a large bank preparing for the installation of a new loans management package. That package was developed using a very powerful code development tool. One of the best tools I have ever found -- before or since. It was capable of doubling the speed of a developer. In fact, for some environments the improvement was four or five times! Unfortunately, it was as capable of developing poor code as it was of developing good code. And of course, no one said you had to use the tool properly, or to its full capability.

The builders of the package were known for attempting to "leave the fold" as it were. In one instance, they spent six person-years (and one actual year) trying to develop a new module using Delphi. Two sales representatives from the development tool company were able to develop the core of the new module in one week. Not a normal situation, but with a customer of that importance you do almost anything to save the business. They were also known for not understanding how to use the development tool.

Okay so far? Then let's go back to the bank. I was engaged to re-think the strategy behind the purchase of the solution. Specifically, the bank had hired the package manufacturer to create and install middleware to translate between the bank's customer list and the package. Understandable from a pure need point of view but somewhat foolish given that the bank already had middleware capable of doing that, the software company had a middleware module capable of doing it, and the coding of a custom version was trivial. Not to mention the fact the package manufacturer had a poor reputation for custom development.

Needless to say, my boss at the time was right to question the wisdom of the decision.

However, in the process of reviewing the decision, I had the dubious pleasure of interviewing the company managers responsible for the decision. It became very obvious, very quickly why the decision had been made.

The managers wanted someone to blame. They were frightened of the risks. They wanted to transfer the risk to someone else. In fact, they were so frightened of the risk that they came very close to eliminating the risk -- but not in their favor. While the project did eventually deliver, it cannot be said to have succeeded. It was some two years late in delivery, well over budget and had enough holes in the coding to drive a Mack truck through.

The managers had been so focused on the wrong definition of risk that they had put the whole project at risk.

Risk is neither good nor bad ... unless you are a project manager going broke on headache tablets. It simply is a fact of life.

Unfortunately, we've been using the word improperly for so long that, like the managers in my story, we become frightened as soon as the word is mentioned.

The mathematical definition of risk is any probability less than 1 but greater than 0. In other words, anything that isn't certain. So winning the lottery is a risk event. For that matter, having a job or being paid is a risk situation. So is having an accident or being struck by lightning. In fact, death is one of the few certainties in life. And that usually is a negative.

The reason that project managers consider risk a negative is because it's one more thing that needs managing and it makes projects less certain. In other words, it means more work!

Risk management is all about identifying the event, the probability, the key indicators and the effect of that event, and then developing a strategy to get the most out of the situation. That may mean exploiting the risk event, overcoming the effect, enhancing the effect, increasing the risk or decreasing the probabilities.

But however you chose to react, it represents one of the top three tasks that a project manager needs to concentrate on.

The Risk Analysis

Risk Analysis is the planning portion of Risk Management. It consists of identifying the possible risk events, evaluating their risk or probability of occurrence and determining a strategy. This strategy may involve avoiding the event, reducing the effect, accepting the effect, assigning the effect to someone else or increasing the probability of the event. This last is important because you will want to encourage the occurrence of any positive event.

Additionally, Risk Analysis includes the evaluation of the various costs associated with the risk event. This can include both the costs involved in avoiding or encouraging the event. It can also include the costs associated with the event if nothing is done, or if something is done. There is also what the cost will be if the event occurs regardless of our best efforts. And it can involve costs that become part of the project budget, part of the project reserve or part of the company's reserve.

Of course, not all risk events need to be managed. The project manager can ignore some events until they occur. Others need a mitigation strategy but not an avoidance or encouragement strategy. Still others will need insurance or an avoidance or encouragement strategy. Much of the direction for this decision will be found in the Risk Management documents discussed in Chapter 3. However, one of the documents flowing from the Risk Analysis is the Risk Strategy or guidance documents. This is typically a completed version of a boilerplate document.

In addition to the general risk strategy document(s) it is also important to create a risk log. This log often includes both a detailed document and a summary document. However, you decide to document the risks you will need to include:

1. Risk Id.
2. Event Description
3. Warning Signs
4. Risk/Probability
   4.a. Before Avoidance
   4.b. After Avoidance
5. Unique Occurrence
6. Absolute Exposure
   6.a. Before Mitigation
   6.b. After Mitigation
7. Risk Exposure
   7.a. Before Mitigation
   7.b. After Mitigation
8. Avoidance Strategy
9. Avoidance Cost
10. Mitigation Strategy
11. Mitigation Cost

Like virtually everything in the project plan, you will need to link back to the specific risk. The "Risk Id." provides a unique key to the specific risk event. This key can be either numeric, or complex depending on the needs and style of the organization.

Of course, the event itself doesn't have a unique key (it's an artificial key). In its place, an "Event Description" is a human readable description of the risk event.

One of the most important elements to risk management is the identification of the event as it occurs. The "Warning Signs" is a description of how the project manager will determine that the risk event has occurred or is going to occur. The project manager can then launch the mitigation strategy.

Of course, not all risk events are equal. Some events are more likely than others. The "Risk/Probability" fields hold the risk or probability of the risk event occurring. However, your organization will determine how you complete this field. Many organizations do not use percentages. Instead, they use a range or class of probabilities. For example a common method is ranking risks as "A, B, C or D" where A is very likely, B is likely and so on.

A project manager designs the avoidance strategy to either reduce risk or to reduce the effect (exposure). Or, of course, to increase the risk if the exposure is a good thing. Unfortunately, no strategy is perfect and risk will never go to zero (or to one if it is a positive exposure). There is always some level of risk. For this reason there are two "Risk/Probability" fields. The first is the "Before Avoidance" field. This is used for the unmodified risk. The second field is the "After Avoidance" field. This is used for the remaining risk.

Similarly, not all risks are exclusive. Some risks will occur only once during the project's life. For example, the loss of a specific key team member is a one time or unique occurrence. On the other hand, rain is not unique. It can occur many times during the same project. The "Unique Occurrence" field can be used to identify unique risks. It can also be used as an indication of the frequency of a particular risk event. In any case, its purpose is to differentiate between repeating and non-repeating risks events.

One of the reasons that risk has a bad name is that it exposes the organization to loss -- or gain. Frequently this gets confused and the potential loss amount is perceived as risk. In fact, this amount is the "Absolute Exposure" not the risk. Of course, this can be negative (i.e. a loss) or it can be positive (i.e. a gain).

Similar to the elimination of risk, it is almost impossible for the project manager to design a solution which eliminates any exposure. The best that can be hoped for is to reduce the exposure to a minimum. In fact, in some strategies the exposure remains constant. However, generally the project manager will develop a mitigation strategy to reduce the effect of the risk event. For this reason it is important to capture the unadjusted exposure ("Before Mitigation") as well as the exposure after all efforts have been taken ("After Mitigation").

Strictly speaking, it isn't necessary to store the "Risk Exposure". After all, it is just the risk multiplied by the exposure. But because this is a manual document, it is easier to calculate the values when the entry is made rather than when the information is retrieved. For the same reason as with the risk and the exposure it is necessary to store two versions of the field. The first is the risk multiplied by the exposure before anything is done ("Before Mitigation"). The second is the value after everything in the strategy is complete ("After Mitigation").

As I've mentioned up to this point there are two strategies that the project manager needs to develop. The first of these, the "Avoidance Strategy" is intended to reduce the risk or reduce the cost associated with the event. Of course in the case of a positive exposure, you will want to design an "Avoidance Strategy" that encourages the event. In either case, the "Avoidance Strategy" will be implemented within the project. This field allows the project manager to record the strategy.

Any strategy will have a cost of implementation. Avoidance is no different. The project manager should track this cost as the "Avoidance Cost". It forms one part of the cost of the project just as the tasks in the avoidance strategy form part of the project.

No matter how good the avoidance strategy, there is always a chance of the risk event taking place. That's when the "Mitigation Strategy" kicks in. The "Mitigation Strategy" allows the effect of the risk event to be mitigated or reduced. This field allows the project manager to record how the project team should react if the event occurs.

In most cases, there is a cost to mitigating the effects of the event. This cost is estimated in the "Mitigation Cost".

Chapter 9

The Scheduling Stream

One of my first projects was for a manager who was one of those minimalist go-getters. You know the ones that don't understand it takes time to predict the future. And no matter what estimate you give, he believes that you can do it for 25% less. I, being young and foolish, didn't realize that just because he didn't want to see the full plan didn't mean that I didn't need to create one. After all, he had been a project manager too. And as boss he should have known what he was doing.

The first time I sat down and planned the project properly and completely despite being rushed. Of course, I rushed some elements in order to produce a complete plan. As a result, my planning wasn't as good as it could be. After being raked over the coals for delivering a full project plan, I decided to follow his lead and only deliver a schedule. The next two projects worked out okay. There was a slight delay but at least it was close. It was also a case of the luck of the Irish.

Unfortunately, that wasn't the case with try number four. Again I only did the schedule and called that the plan. But this time everything went wrong. Somewhere around triple the original budget, my brand new boss suggested that we had a personality conflict. He also suggested that I would be happier elsewhere. I later learned that my old boss had several projects fail. Mine wasn't the worst.

There is a common opinion amongst those who aren't familiar with project management that a project plan is the project schedule. That the entire plan is contained within the milestones document.

As we've seen so far, the project plan actually consists of much more than just the schedule.

But there's a reason why that opinion is so pervasive. Everything else in the plan re-appears during the scheduling stream. It is in the scheduling stream that all the elements that make up a project come together.

So what is the scheduling stream? It's the stream where the project manager identifies all the tasks associated with the previous streams. Where he, or she, describes all the tasks to create the product. Where the project manager describes and schedules all the required materials and services. Where the project manager allocates and requests people to perform the tasks that make up the project. Where the due dates and durations are estimated and scheduled.

In short, it's the stream that determines what will be done and when.

The WBS

When you create a product, one of the documents you create is the bill of materials. This document deconstructs the product into a number of assemblies, sub-assemblies and eventually pieces and parts. Its purpose is to ensure that all the parts necessary to manufacture the product are available.

The Work Breakdown Structure or WBS performs much the same purpose. But in this case, the pieces and parts are the tasks involved in performing the project.

The decomposition diagram known as the WBS helps to ensure that you take into account all the tasks that make up the project. It also is the base for preparing estimates and scheduling the project.

Typically, the WBS consists of a diagram and a detailed list of the tasks on the WBS. The diagram is a standard decomposition diagram typically labeled with the WBS Id. and the Task Title. The detailed list of the tasks is a separate sheet containing any other related information for each of the tasks or work packages (task assemblies). Typically, it contains the following:

1. WBS Id.
2. Description
3. Task Title
4. Outputs and Deliverables
5. Requirements Identifier(s).
6. Quality Requirement Identifier(s)
7. Due Date

The "WBS Id." acts as the unique identifier for the project task or work package. In fact, it should consist of a structured number indicating the location of the task within the WBS hierarchy. For example, 3.2.1 would indicate that the task was the first task under the second work package in the third group of tasks. Of course, the exact structure will vary depending on the structure of the project. It should also be noted that some organizations enforce a different numbering method. As long as the result is a unique value it doesn't matter.

Every organization has a different version of what should be included in the "Description" of the task. In fact, the format of the description depends largely on the nature of the task. Some tasks will need a long description, while others need only the barest of descriptions. However, whatever the decision, there should always be enough information for the person doing the task to understand what they need to do. In some cases, it may be necessary to include the description as a separate form in order to provide a second layer of detail.

Unfortunately, a description of the task won't fit on the typical WBS diagram. Instead we need to use a "Task Title". There is some variation in the title formats typically used. However, it should follow a verb-subject structure if possible. For example, one might use "Build Wall" as a "Task Title".

As we discovered back in the discussion on The Task Assignment Cycle in Chapter 2, a quality assignment requires us to describe "What" we expect the task to produce. This description forms the "Outputs and Deliverables" field.

Back in the requirements discussion in Chapter 7, I stated that an important concept was the traceability of requirements. We need to be able to prove that a requirement was met. Equally, we need to identify the requirement in order to answer any questions that arise. The "Requirements Identifier(s)" field satisfies both these needs.

This is very similar to the "Quality Requirement Identifier(s)". Essentially this is just the same field applied to the quality requirements rather than the general needs.

In order to meet the overall project it is sometimes necessary that individual tasks must complete prior to a specific "Due Date". Typically, this is set during the scheduling process. However, occasionally situations outside of the project determine the required date. For this reason, the "Due Date" field is included in the WBS document at this point.

The Materials Analysis

Project managers sometimes think of projects as driven by time and energy. We forget that not all projects depend solely on the people who perform the work. Some types of projects have large material components. An IT implementation project, for example, may require the ordering of a hundred new PCs. A construction project needs wood, steel, pipe and electric cable ordered.

The tasks within this process focus on identifying the materials needed to complete the work. In effect, they identify the work packages to be fulfilled by applying the materials procurement procedures.

When the process is complete, you can expect to have a number of tasks to add to the WBS. In addition, you will have a list containing the following information:

1. Materials Id.
2. Description
3. Target Date
4. Lead Time
5. Possible Suppliers
6. Estimated Budget

Some organizations refer to the "Materials Id." as the "Product Id.". However, most organizations use the Purchase Requisition Number as this field. This allows for purchasing the same materials throughout the life of the project. Each purchase is then considered as a unique purchasing event. And the number is tracked throughout the purchasing system.

It is important when ordering materials to know what to order. This is the purpose behind the "Description" field. The project manager is able to describe whatever information the buyer requires in order to purchase the item. Of course, sometimes the "Description" field is not sufficient. In that case, it is not unusual to produce a more detailed description form.

The project manager and project team will assign most of the dates during the scheduling step. However, sometimes it is necessary to identify a "Target Date" based on external factors. Typically, the material must arrive by this date.

One of the common concepts in purchasing is "Lead Time". Essentially this is the time it takes from identification of the need to the product being available. Included are time allowances for such things as requesting an RFP, mailing the purchase order and shipping from receiving to where the product will be consumed. Your organization's purchasing department should be able to supply reasonable lead times.

Frequently the materials purchased for a project are unique to that project. In order to assist the buyers, the project team often provides a list of "Possible Suppliers". This is not always required. Nor is it always available.

Of course, every purchase has a cost involved. In order to assist the budgeting process, it is important to determine an "Estimated Budget" for the materials.

Because this document will end up being an input document to the purchasing process, many organizations already have fixed document requirements. For example, they may require a purchase requisition for each of the materials purchases (i.e. each line on the list) or even a purchase order. Or they may have an existing form of the list (purchase requisitions usually fit this category). In any case, this document, more than any other, is subject to the organization's needs, history and desires.

The People Analysis

Just as a project needs to purchase the right materials, projects need to get the right people assigned. These people can be from internal sources or outsourced to contractors or freelancers. The people analysis determines what types of people the project needs and who is going to assume responsibility for the various tasks. It also determines the tasks the project needs to carry out in order to obtain the services of those people.

Projects are all about the people involved. The project manager's first task is to get the individuals involved focused on the job at hand and then get out of their way. And the best way to do that is to choose the right people for the job. It tends to make things much easier if you don't have to mash people into the wrong shaped hole.

Three core forms are generated from the people analysis stream. These are:

1. The Responsibility Assignment Matrix (RAM)
2. The Project Team Organization Chart
3. The Project Team Contact List

The Responsibility Assignment Matrix actually has a number of different names. However, almost all of them have the same acronym -- RAM. And most project managers know it by its acronym. There are several different versions as each player adds what they feel is important. However, whatever version you use, the purpose of the RAM is to identify the various individuals who participate in a task and their role.

The version which I am going to suggest has the tasks listed down the left hand column. The key individuals are listed along the top with their position description.

Because not all the individuals are key, some will be assigned based on who is available when. For these individuals the position description is used. Usually, part of the task is to group these individuals by the position description. So for example, if you need four carpenters assigned by the union on the day of work, you would group them as carpenters.

Where the task and the individual intersect, you enter one of five codes - R for responsible, P for participant, I for information source, S for source (i.e. provider) and O for oversight or manage. Of course, the organization needs to identify its own versions of the codes.

Name	Greg	Paul
Position	IT Manager	Stakeholder Rep.
Analyse	R	P, I
Design	R	I
Program	R	
Test	R,S	O

Figure 3

The result is a table that looks like that shown in Figure 3.

The Project Team Organization Chart is just a standard organization chart. No different from the dozens you've probably seen already. Its purpose is to display the reporting hierarchy in a visual manner. In this case, the term "project team" includes those who will be working during the execution or later phases as well as those responsible for planning. Typically, it will show the position and either the name of the individual or the number of people filling that role. Of course, at this stage, many of the assignments may be tentative. So it is possible that only key team members will appear with a name attached.

The Project Team Contact list is a project team version of the Stakeholder contact list we saw in Chapter 6. In fact, when computerizing the contact lists, it is quite common to combine the lists in the database and then display the two lists separately. The Group field is typically set to Team Member when doing this, to allow selection. However, there are some different requirements. These are typically added to the Stakeholder Contact file. On the other hand, they are only displayed when entering a Team Member.

Having said that, if you were to treat them as independent lists you would require the following information:

1. Team Member Identification
   1.a. Id. Number
   1.b. Name
2. Contact Information
   2.a. Phone Number
   2.b. Fax
   2.c. Email
   2.d. Address
3. Position
4. Reports to

Just as in the generic Stakeholder contact list, there are two fields that are unique to the individual being described. At least in theory.

The first is a unique pointer I call the "Id Number" or occasionally the Member Id. Frequently the Stakeholder Id. is used in order to link both records. This artificial identifier exists because the real world identifier is not unique. I'm referring, of course, to the "Name". I've actually discussed this in Chapter 6. The same situation exists so I'm not going to repeat myself here.

There is one odd element about the identification fields. In many cases, you will begin the project not knowing who will make up the project team. Instead, the project manager identifies key members and positions to fill later. I've discussed this under the RAM discussion amongst other places. There are two philosophies. One says that creation of the team records occurs as part of the assignment process. The other says to create the team records using positions and null individual information. There are arguments on both sides. Both decisions are equally valid. Your organization needs to determine how it will handle this issue.

We also need to keep track of "Contact Information" for this individual. The nature and format of this information is identical to the version in Chapter 6. If you need an explanation of the fields, please re-read the discussion under "The Stakeholder" in Chapter 6.

Of course, team members are on the team in order to provide access to their skills. They therefore fulfill a position within the project. We record that information under the term "Position".

The team is a hierarchy. No matter how self-directed. No matter at what organizational level the team functions. It has a hierarchy. That is why we need to identify the individual's superior within the project. Largely this is the same information found in the Project Team Organization Chart. It just happens to be in a text format rather than a visual format. In theory, it can be left off and the inquiries directed to the Project Team Organization Chart. I just feel that the advantages in flexibility and availability are well worth the small amount of effort involved in recording the "Reports to".

The Schedule

The Schedule process is actually a series of tasks ranging from estimation to selecting the dates to use as milestones. All of these tasks point toward determining when people and materials are needed, how long they will be needed, and when the products of the project will be available.

Traditionally, management considers the schedule as the raison d'etre of planning. In fact, as the story I opened this chapter with described, sometimes the schedule is thought to be the whole of the project plan. Almost inevitably, that opinion leads to serious project failure. On the other hand, the schedule is where all the other work comes together in a nice, neat package.

As befits its importance, the schedule documents actually consist of several different documents. In fact, a large number of different tools (i.e. documents) can help the process. Some of these are virtually mandatory. However, my job in this book is not to teach you how to schedule your project. My goal in this book is to identify what documents from planning are required in the project plan manual. So you may find that you actually create a number of extra documents. These should be included in the project manual (of which the project plan manual is a section). However, you may find that your organization demands some of these extra documents be in the project plan manual instead.

Similarly, I am being somewhat naïve and rigid in my definition of the documents. This is especially true in the case of the network diagram and the Gantt Chart. Modern versions of the Gantt Chart (as produced by Microsoft Project for example) are often not, in fact, Gantt Charts. Rather they are a hybrid of the network diagram and a Gantt Chart. For my purposes, I'm going to ignore the fact that you can create a single document to do both tasks by using a modern tool. In the real world where MS Project is ubiquitous, the separation is a matter of how far you have gotten in the entry of information. Since I am writing under the constraint of manual documentation, I am going to keep the two tools separate.

Finally, many organizations require the existence of a detailed work document. This is a single form for each task containing all of the information on that task. This is a very good idea. However, it isn't mandatory -- especially in a light project, so I've left it out.

There are four major documents required for the project plan from the scheduling process.

The first is the Network Diagram. This is simply a map of how each of the tasks is related to each of the other tasks. Can two tasks be done concurrently or does one need to be completed before the other? There are many different versions of this document. In theory, at least, there are two distinct types. Properly speaking, these are referred to as Activity on Arrow (AOA) and Activity on Node (AON). In practice there are a number of different names for each of these depending largely on the style and background of the creator. Often the differences between these formats have more to do with the marketing of consulting services and using the Queen's English or a local patois than with project management.

One purpose of the Network Diagram is to document task precedence in the project. Another purpose is to determine the Critical Path ... that is the series of tasks which determine the length of the project. Finally, the last purpose is to determine which tasks need to be done, and in which order.

Once the order of the project task has been determined, it is necessary to map that order on a calendar. That is the job of the Gantt Chart. It also explains why the hybrid Gantt is so common.

Next, a task list needs to be created to document the tasks and certain critical information. In the real world, adding a number of fields to the WBS list is the solution. I described this list earlier in this chapter. Specifically this process adds the following fields to create an Enhanced WBS:

1. Responsibility
2. Estimated Duration
3. Scheduled End Date
4. Earliest Start Date
5. Dependencies

The "Responsibility" field identifies "Who" we are expecting to assign the "Responsibility" for completion of the task.

The "Estimated Duration" field contains our best guess of how long each of the tasks will take to complete a process within the project. For my purposes, I am only going to identify a single value. However, depending on the needs of the organization, it may be necessary to hold multiple values based on most likely, lowest and highest. This information helps to determine a good budget.

In order for the project to be delivered on time, every task has a "Scheduled End Date". This is the latest date that the task can be completed by without impacting the final delivery date of the project.

Unless a task is on the critical path, there is some flexibility in when it can start. The last start date can be calculated from the Scheduled End Date and the Estimated Duration. I could include the lag and the lead times but it's easier just to record the "Earliest Start Date".

In theory, it isn't necessary to indicate the "Dependencies" for a task. After all, that's the purpose of the Network Diagram (or Gantt if you are using the hybrid version). However, just as I included the Reports To field to make life easier, I do the same with this field.

This list forms the basis for the fourth list. The final list is a selection of items from the Enhanced WBS. Specifically, we are going to identify the project milestones in a Milestones list. For this, we need to identify what tasks mark milestones. We then need to add a Milestone task (a zero duration task which simply marks the delivery of the milestone). At the same time, we need to create a list containing:

1. Item being Delivered
2. Date Scheduled

While in theory, a milestone is defined as a zero duration task, in the real world a milestone is key point in the project. This is normally defined as the delivery of a particular element in the project -- the "Item being Delivered". Delivery of this sub-product on time means that the whole of the project is most likely on line to complete when scheduled.

The "Date Scheduled" is simply the "Scheduled End Date" for the task. This marks the last date for the delivery of the "Item Being Delivered".

Chapter 10

The Cost Stream

In project management theory, every project comes down to its budget. After all, the three great criteria are budget, time and quality. Often project management texts give examples of how to balance the three while keeping the scope constant. Most frequently, these examples involve the trade-off between budget or cost, and time.

In the real world, many project managers are not required to work in terms of dollars. This has some advantages in terms of responsibility and complexity. However, it also reduces the ability to manipulate costs in order to improve time or quality. Effectively, by not including costs you are presuming that all resources produce the same quality product in the same period of time. A presumption which is obviously not correct given that the measured difference in productivity between a senior programmer and a junior programmer is 500 %.

Do not mistake this situation for the project manager not being responsible for the budget. The project manager still has a budget which needs to be managed to. However, rather than measuring the budget and expenses in terms of dollars, the measure is in terms of person-hours.

Money is simply a way of measuring different resources using a single measure. A way of comparing apples and oranges, as it were. The requirement to keep the costs within predictions remains. The measure simply changes.

The Cost Plan

In essence a budget is simply a cost plan expressed in terms of a particular base -- dollars preferably, person-hours frequently. It describes how and where you anticipate spending resources.

Just as the schedule plans for time and the quality analysis plans for quality, so the budget plans for the spending of resources. The budget describes your plan for spending money (or person-hours).

A budget is essentially a general ledger containing estimated values rather than actual values. All general ledgers consist of two parts -- a list of detailed transactions and a summary listing. A budget is no different. The big differences are that in a budget, estimated amounts are entered and only the total is entered for each budgeted cycle (e.g. month, quarter or week).

In an operation, spending takes place over a fiscal year. Typically, there is a cycle of spending which is described in terms of months. With a project, spending takes place over the life of the project. Depending on the length of the project, it may be necessary to measure spending cycles in different terms. The fiscal year is an obvious cycle, as is a month. But typically reporting on projects takes place on a weekly or bi-weekly basis. So weekly budgeting is also common. Your organization will determine the minimum cycles that must be accounted for.

As a result you will most likely need to produce two reports. One report is common to all projects. This is a summary of the budget for the life of the project. It is this report which is used in the project plan. However, you should also produce a detailed budget. This can be kept in the project plan manual as an appendix. For some organizations this is a requirement. However, in some cases, the detailed budget is relegated to the project manual. This is a case where the information needs for a sponsor varies from that needed by the project manager.

The summary budget should consist of a list of the following with only one entry per description:

1. Account Id.
2. Description
3. Estimated Amount
4. Budgeted Amount
5. Reserve Amount

The "Account Id." is an artificial unique identifier. Typically, it corresponds to the general ledger account number. Doing so allows for much easier recording and matching of expense transactions when the project is in the execution phases.

The "Description" is effectively the name of the account. It should describe the reason for the spending.

There are three amounts required for the budget -- the estimated amount, the budgeted amount and the reserve amount.

Because project planning is an attempt to predict the future, projects work through estimates. Estimates are key to understanding the prediction process. It is important therefore to maintain some form of recording and quality measurement on the estimation process.

However, for governance purposes, the necessary amount is the budget. Typically, this is related to the estimate. After all, it starts out from the estimate. However, the budget is adjusted for a number of reasons which are not related to the estimate. It is up to the project manager to spend or not spend the project budget amount. One of the tasks during project closure is to release unspent budget amounts back to the organization.

The final amount is the reserve. Reserve amounts require approval in order to access them. Typically, reserves are limited to risk items. Specifically, there are two types of reserve. The first is limited to the life of the project. Often this is included directly in the budget. In any case, it is written off when the project finishes. The second is more complex.

Certain exposures, such as estimation variation, are not related to the project per se. Rather they are related to the portfolio of projects currently being undertaken by the organization. Think of it as self-insurance. The company needs to identify how much they need to reserve in case of the occurrence of an event. Reserve for bad debts is an example from operations. No one account can be determined in advance as being a bad debt. However, the organization knows from experience that a certain percentage of its outstanding debt will remain unpaid.

The detailed budget is an expansion of the summary budget. Detail does not refer to the number of items included, but rather to the time involved.

In order to create the detailed budget it is necessary to add an "Estimated Date" field to the summary accounts fields. The entry should be based on the date the expense is estimated to occur. However, this entry remains a summary entry. This is why the early discussion on reporting cycles was important. The actual date used should correspond to the reporting cycle and there should be only one entry per reporting cycle.

What's In The Project Plan Manual At This Point?

The cost stream is the last of the streams to be completed. You are now ready to forward your response to the sponsor for approval.

At this point your project plan manual will consist of:

1. A title page
2. Executive Summary
3. Detailed Plan (Strategy) (One paragraph each):
   3.a. Overall Strategy
   3.b. Scope Statement
   3.c. Project Milestones
   3.d. Major risks
   3.e. Summary Budget
   3.f. Major Stakeholders (Structure)
   3.g. Stakeholder Reaction Strategy
   3.h. Communications Strategy
   3.i. Requirements Strategy
   3.j. Project Change Strategy
   3.k. Quality Strategy
   3.l. Risk Management Strategy
4. Appendices:
   4.a. Portfolio Detail Record (usually called a project request form)
   4.b. Portfolio Business Case (the justification)
   4.c. Project Charter (this is sometimes used as the title section)
   4.d. One-page descriptions of the standard project processes.
   4.d.1. Project Changes
   4.d.2. Materials Procurement

4.d.3. Personnel Procurement

4.d.4. Human Resource variations

4.d.5. Project Risk

4.e. The Stakeholder Communications stream

4.e.1. Stakeholders Contact List

4.e.2. Stakeholder Reaction Analysis

4.e.3. Stakeholder Communications Analysis

4.f. The Requirements Stream

4.f.1. Detailed Requirements

4.f.2. Requirements Log (Summary)

4.f.3. Scope Statement

4.g. Quality Management

4.g.1. Quality Strategy

4.g.2. Quality Requirements

4.h. The Risks Stream

4.h.1. Risk Strategy

4.h.2. Risk Log

4.i. The Scheduling Stream

4.i.1. WBS Diagram

4.i.2. Extended WBS/Task List

4.i.3. Materials Procurement List

4.i.4. RAM

4.i.5. Project Team Organization Chart

4.i.6. Project Team Contact List

4.i.7. Network Diagram

4.i.8. GANTT Chart

4.j. The Cost Management Stream

4.J.1. Detailed Budget

4.j.2. Summary Budget

Chapter 11

Approvals

In many ways, we have finished the actual project plan. We now have a plan and the documents to support that plan. Our plan is the response to the original request. In effect, it is the prediction of what will happen when we attempt to achieve the scope given what we currently know.

At this point we now have a document which can be given to management as the project plan.

Of course, request and response are only two of the tasks involved. The third, is the approval or permission to proceed. It is not unusual for the approval to be withdrawn and the process repeated as the results, timing and costs are negotiated.

Hopefully at some point, the project plan will be approved or "green lighted". At that point the approvals document will be created. That document is a very simple document containing the following information:

1. Project Id.
2. Sponsor
3. Project Manager
4. Approved Budget
5. Limits of Authority
6. Approving Signature

In theory, several of these fields are not required if the form is part of the project manual. However, typically, the form is actually an email. Often it goes from the project manager to the sponsor to document a verbal authorization. Of course, this isn't what should happen, but it is what often happens.

In fact, in some organizations, approval occurs prior to the response. If at all possible, this should be avoided as it puts everyone at risk. If you think about it -- approval before the response means that the sponsor is approving what the sponsor just gave to the project manager. A definite case of redundant duplication.

The "Project Id." is the identifier used throughout the project planning manual (and later the project manual) to uniquely identify the project.

The "Sponsor" and the "Project Manager" are the two key management representatives on the project. The presumption here is that both parties are assigned to the project. The "Sponsor" represents management and portfolio governance and the "Project Manager" takes responsibility for project governance. In the real world, it is typically the "Sponsor" who authorizes the project. However, for our purposes I am not making that presumption.

The "Approved Budget" and the "Limits of Authority" both define what the project manager is authorized to do. Generally speaking the "Approved Budget" should match the project budget in the cost portion of the project plan. If it doesn't the project plan needs to be recast in order to meet the budget. In essence, this represents a negative authorization masquerading as a green-light.

While the person approving the project should actually sign the form, in the real world, only third party projects get signed. If at all possible, some form of acknowledgement of the approval should be captured, as it is important to the project manager. Even an email confirming that the sponsor has approved the project plan verbally is better than nothing at all.

Chapter 12

Conclusion

There is a tendency when working on a project to downgrade the importance of the project plan. In IT it's called the WICCA effect -- Why Isn't Charlie Coding Anything. As managers, we don't want people to sit around and talk about doing. We want people to be doing.

As a project manager we need to overcome that tendency. The project plan is a key element in the governance of the project. In many ways, for anything except a trivial project, it represents the success or failure of the project. Jumping into the actual work prematurely is one of the worst mistakes that an organization can make.

On the other hand, becoming locked into "analysis paralysis" is also not wise. It too guarantees failure.

The trick is to understand that the project planning process consists of a set of specific tasks, focused on a specific result. It is never perfect. There is never perfect information available. The result will never be perfect.

But establishing a baseline, provides the beginnings of useful governance.

From here, the project plan can be adjusted as more information is obtained. Tasks will be added. Tasks will disappear. Change is inevitable.

But the project plan -- as imperfect as it is -- is the base that the information grows on.

Where To Go From Here?

Once approved the project plan manual becomes the guiding force for the project. It defines what will be done, when it will be done and, most importantly, why it will be done. It provides guidance to decisions around the changes. It provides guidance to the performance of the project. And it provides guidance for the reporting of performance.

With the full project manual, two copies of the project plan manual are needed. The first becomes the original baseline. The second becomes the current plan. As changes occur, this plan is corrected.

Several of the elements also become seed documents to help track the project as it progresses. For example, the schedule is repeated multiple times -- as the original baseline, the current baseline and the actual -- each showing different information.

Offer - Free Templates

Back in chapter 1, I explained that a picture was worth a thousand words. Or in this case roughly twenty six thousand. Now the normal solution is to add an appendix containing the templates and a sample project plan manual.

Unfortunately, this book is intended to be published on the Kindle. Besides, why should I ask you to recreate my forms?

So I've created a set of downloadable templates, plus a sample project plan. If you go to

http://store.glendford.com/extras/htdpp

you will have the opportunity to download those templates and plan. You will need to enter your name, email, a password and a coupon code. The coupon code is

PRINTPLAN

You'll receive an email with directions for downloading the templates. Please ensure that you check your spam folder and then whitelist (always accept) mail from that address. I won't overload you with emails and I won't give your email to anyone else. What I will do is let you have advance notice of any new books (including special premiums) and occasionally send you news and articles related to project management or business management.

Last Thoughts

One of the greatest gifts that anyone can give another is the gift of their time. It doesn't matter if the receiver is a child, a spouse or a complete stranger. Time is the one asset that truly is limited in supply and unlimited in value.

Whenever a writer sits down to create a book like this one there is always a sense of trepidation. Will the information be of use to the reader? Will the reader be interested? Will the reader become bored? Will the reader take the time to read the book? Will the reader actually use the information?

I want to thank you for taking the time to read this book of mine. I hope you have found it both enlightening and enjoyable.

Most of all I hope that you will apply what you have learned and that you will find your time was well spent.

I would like to ask one further favor of you. Could you take five minutes to help other readers?

Other readers rely on your opinions when choosing which books to spend their precious time reading. Writers like me rely on your feedback to improve their writing and to know what topics to write about next.

If you enjoyed this book, please express your rating and opinions on Amazon. Amazon provides a facility for rating and reviewing on the page where you purchased this book. You can reach the review page by going to the bottom of http://www.amazon.com/dp/B005YV7BTS and selecting the 'write a customer review' button.

I enjoy speaking with other project managers and especially with my readers so please feel free to contact me through the contact form available at my publisher's site http://TrainingNOW.ca or the one at my own website http://GlenDFord.com. While you are at my site, feel free to check out my blog. It contains many of my thoughts on project management, innovation and business management for entrepreneurs.

Good luck and happy project planning.

Glen Ford
Mississauga, Ontario, Canada

How to Write Your Own How-To EBook in 24 Hours or Less: The information products secret revealed!

How to Document a Project Plan: What you need to know to design a project management plan quickly and easily

How to Blog for Money: 9 strategies to get your blog earning money online and off

Writer's Block Demolition: Finding the time to write, keeping writing, and finish YOUR book

101 Writing Tweets: 101 tips and tweets about writing how-to books for the Kindle

As Glen Douglas

How To Build A Raised Garden Bed

With Paul Benson

101 Limericks About Public Speaking

Glen Ford

Glen Ford was formerly the Chief Operating Officer/Chief Information Officer and a co-founder with VProz Inc. He is a serial entrepreneur having set up the internet training company TrainingNOW and its subsidiaries as well as providing consulting services for startups in Debt Counseling, Software and Payment Processing. He has been principal of his own project management consultancy for over 11 years. During that time he has alternated his clients between government, the big banks and small to medium companies. Prior to that he spent 10 years working for the Canadian Standards Association and 10 years alternating between large distribution and manufacturing companies. He also worked for a very successful HVAC firm. Glen is now training, writing, coaching, and consulting on project management and related entrepreneurship topics including the implementation of PMOs and methodologies. You can reach him directly through his website http://www.GlenDFord.com.

Glen is active in the business community as a member of The Project Management Institute (PMI) Lakeshore Chapter and a former training director for BNI Eagles Chapter of Business Network International (BNI). Glen is also an active supporter of charity including Scouts Canada (3rd Erin Mills Scouts). Glen holds a BSc from McMaster University in Hamilton, an MCPM from York University (Schulich), and a PMP (Project Management Professional) designation.

TrainingNOW

TrainingNOW is a training *Training* and publishing company located in Mississauga and Burlington, Ontario, Canada. It provides specialized web hosting services for companies seeking to deliver "how to" education over the web. It also publishes and sells "how to" books and training materials in digital, print and other media. Through its subsidiaries LearningCreators and ContentCreators it provides training on how to write your own book and, provides custom training material development including books.

Glen Ford is available as a trainer, speaker, coach, or consultant. You can find more information on his courses, and services at http://GlenDFord.com

You can find more information on training courses, books, and publishing your own books at http://TrainingNOW.ca

You can email the writer through either site.

www.ingramcontent.com/pod-product-compliance
Lightning Source LLC
Chambersburg PA
CBHW061309220326
41599CB00026B/4805